© 2019

Written by: Don Beaudoin Jr. (P/N)

Contributing Editors: Christine W. (FirstEditing.com), T.M. and Others

Foreword: Daniel Carmody

Data Researcher: Matt Flynn

New Buffalo Nickel Publishing & Holdings, LLC

All rights reserved.

Published with Amazon.com

ISBN: 978-09994821-2-4

TABLE OF CONTENTS

PART I: My Letter to Trump

PART II: Facilitating Better Economics

PART III: Cultural Change & Economics

PART IV Our Future Potential

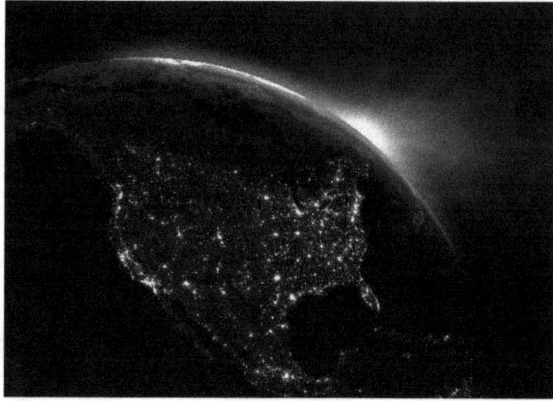

PART I

My Letter to Trump

"Liberty and Justice for All."

-Francis Bellamy

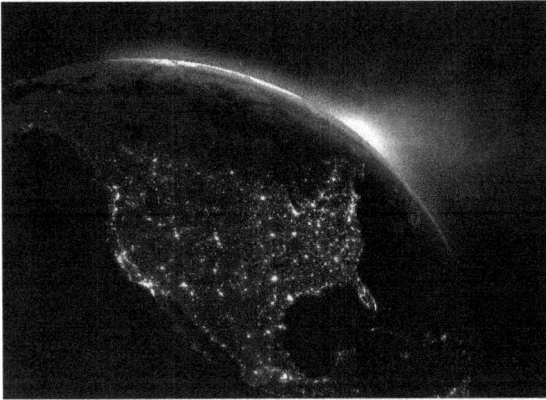

FOREWORD

About the Author & The Book

Don Beaudoin is a decorated military combat veteran with moderate libertarian political and economic views. He served in the U.S. Marine Corps from 2001 to 2009 and did two tours to the Middle East as a helicopter pilot in 2005 and 2007. Since leaving the military, he obtained a master's in business administration and has worked within manufacturing for several years using statistics to help improve processes and systems. He hopes this book, embedded with the lessons he has learned from an education of many sorts, and from brushing elbows with America's finest fighting men and women, CEO's, Congressmen, and Generals, can help bring some perspective to the internal cultural and political conflict occurring in the United States. The purpose of this book is to bring a more data-based objective understanding of the real economic influencers affecting Americans and to put the focus where it belongs, America's future.

I have known Don for 27 years. Even in middle school, discussions of global significance were a common occurrence. We were two poor kids growing up in a small town on the edge of the deep south. Combined with this we both came from family backgrounds that were challenging. So, we understood the plight of kids who must fend for themselves early on.

Education and the military were our common outlets. Over the course of the last 25 years, we've learned just how great a country America is because of the opportunity it can provide for those even of the humblest beginnings. Both Don and I were in high school JROTC and wanted to see the world. We both eventually went on to serve in the combat zones of the Middle East. There's nothing like having a friend for life that is also familiar with the common acronyms so prevalent in military service. We know the feeling of being part of something greater than ourselves. That's just what this book is about. It's Don's understanding of how we are part of the greatest country on earth and should act like it. His plea is to put politics aside and see the bigger picture for our prosperity and freedoms to remain strong.

Don doesn't intend to get involved in politics other than offering the advice he can give. He does not have the wealth or ambition to personally get involved. In his opinion, the world of politics has become too divisive. Our news media stations now make a show out of attacking the personal faults of our politicians rather than measuring them on their current political views, the value of their ideas, or their leadership abilities. This is why the author of the book used a pen name. He doesn't care for the media hype that lacks the intellectual capacity to change systems for the better. It takes work to do that, not just words. His bottom line is that he hopes some of the recommendations within the book will be considered by U.S. leadership to promote positive change.

In 2011, Don wrote Mr. Donald J. Trump and asked him to run for President of the United States as an Independent in a letter promoting the representation of Americans who consider themselves moderates instead of extreme. Currently, he does not support all of President Trump's policies. Instead, he presents the trends in the last few decades in a way that lets an American voter decide whether President Trump could be an agent of change during a second term in office or not. Could President Trump challenge his own elite class's influences on America's workers? It all has to do with the potential for change relative to the other alternatives for the Presidency. It's not really about President Trump, it's about the *Big Picture*.

Ultimately, the argument given within this book is that even if you despise President Trump's controversial words used on his twitter account or his method of attacks he uses against his political or economic opponents, you should give this book a read to understand what is really going on in America causing economic and cultural tension. Then let your conscious decide who to vote for in 2020. What is evident from reading this book is that the current establishment's (both Democrats & Republicans) consistent promotion of rigged economic policy is hurting America's working classes.

Don's arguments are backed by historical economic trends, a deciphering of U.S. domestic and foreign policy, and a very strong understanding of the special interests' actions that have occurred in the last few decades. He also is able to show that our legislatures were asleep at the wheel allowing predatorial policy to be systematically injected into our laws. While doing so, both Democratic and Republican legislatures ran cover for special interests groups by focusing the political discourse on cultural and religious differences between Americans. While some of the legislative changes have been good over the years particularly those that promoted equal opportunity and greater access to housing and healthcare, it was mixed with status quo economic legislation promoting the drain on lower-income and middle-class Americans. The legislation has made it extremely difficult for the poor and middle classes to survive economically without two or more jobs per household. The legislatures that participated in selling out the American people were awarded with long careers in Washington

4

D.C. Our lower House of Representatives who are the voice of the people stopped representing us and instead, traded their integrity and duty to the American people for job security.

This book is over 170 pages with graphs and charts to help illustrate the author's data-driven analysis of the latest hot topic issues in American politics, economics, and culture. No other author tells the story of the increasing squeeze over half of Americans feel almost daily than Don Beaudoin. He does it through roundtable like chapters that are a discussion between himself and all the counterpoints he can think of. This way of book writing is exactly what our country needs to avoid the fundamental process failures occurring in America today. It hits the misnomers one by one with logic-based reasoning and masterfully applied data until the misnomers do not hold water. It then offers potential solutions for a range of issues facing America today. If we are to be logical, we must agree that our last 40 years' of politics in America has wielded us three common results: the accumulation of wealth for the ultra-wealthy, the depletion of wealth for America's working classes, and an ever-increasing size of the U.S. Federal Government and debt. Is this what we want to continue? This book is the spirit of the truth when it comes to what is going on in America right now with our political parties working together behind the scenes to divide Americans culturally in order to conquer us economically. It shows that special interests groups facilitated by U.S. Democratic and Republican Senates and Houses, the U.S. Supreme Court, and previous U.S. Presidents are selling out America's working classes. I'm proud to be a contributor to a book that can arm Americans, whether they are rich, poor, and of all different backgrounds with the right information prior to the 2020 election.

Daniel Carmody

Friend and Fellow Military Veteran

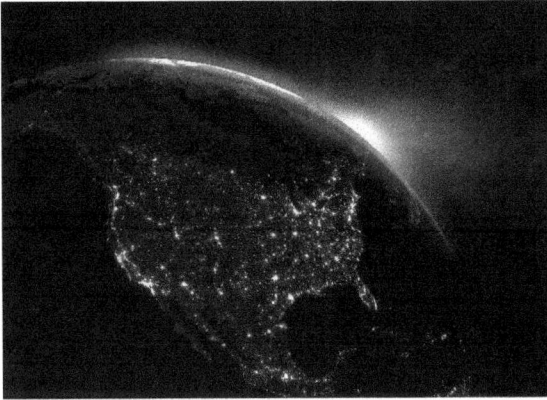

Chapter 1

The Letter: February 25th, 2011

I have always been the type of individual that saw the big picture. Not the big picture I needed to see at any given time to benefit myself, but the big picture that far exceeded any of my control. Some have called me a dreamer to my face. They were right. I excelled in math and science during high school. I attended a military university and was curious about history, politics, religion, and everything else. So, instead of getting a mechanical engineering degree, I switched at the last minute to a political science degree.

After graduation, I was required to attend a pre-flight school course in Pensacola. During the course, a professor who had contacts with the CIA gave the flight students a lecture that included some foreshadowing of an impending second war with Iraq. During one of the lectures, he asked around thirty flight students in attendance if an invasion of Iraq would prove difficult. How my fellow flight students responded that day seared into my memory. It was reminiscent of a scene from *Gone with the Wind* when the southern boys discussed how easily they would "lick" those Yankees. Several of the lieutenants stood up and discussed how the U.S. arsenal would obliterate the Iraqi Army and we would win in days. This being pre-insurgency days in both Afghanistan and Iraq, who was to say any different? Well, I had to say something because I had studied Iraq a bit and I also knew a little bit about the history of the Middle East. I said, as closely as I can remember:

> "Iraq is different from Afghanistan. The Sunnis that support Saddam there have a base of power that's pretty-well established throughout the Middle East. If we go to war with Iraq and remove Saddam, we will destabilize the region and probably end up having to fight more than just the Iraqis and a lot of Americans will likely be killed."

The room was aghast. You could hear a pin drop. Almost the entire room full of lieutenants disagreed. There were several comebacks that vehemently stated I was dead wrong and that I must not have a clue about what U.S. offensive capabilities can do. The students that may have agreed with me kept silent. I didn't say anything else but listened to half a dozen other students tell the class why my point was wrong. Finally, one person did agree. The professor himself. After all the counterarguments, to my surprise, he was more inclined to believe it would prove difficult due to Iraq's potential to balkanize destabilizing the region. After the class, he wanted me to stay and we had a lengthy discussion on why I thought war in Iraq could prove difficult.

I have a selective but good memory when it comes to the motivations or factors behind how people or systems work. That has led me to trying to connect the dots to economics, military, political, and cultural issues. My curiosity has led me to converse with many ranking officials in the Marines Corps, other military branches, our governmental officials, and within the business world over the last 20 years. Did I hear anything classified? Not to my knowledge. Hearing or seeing classified information isn't what has allowed me to assess America's economic and cultural situation. Nor is it how I've come up with potential solutions.

Whatever privileged and top-secret knowledge American officials possess, it clearly hasn't helped America in the last 40 years. So, even if I had been given the opportunity to review classified data or information prior to writing this book, I would have turned down the opportunity for this reason: our officials with the highest clearances and hallways full of bright minds already have access to this stuff. With all of these abundant resources at their disposal, they have nearly bankrupted our country and at the same time only been able to muster stagnant wages for about half of Americans in the last 40 years. While doing so, they have consistently reported Americans are better off (basing their opinions on numeric averages rather than the state of most Americans). Then, they retire in luxury like the top CEO's do, "Welcome to the club my friend."

Over-dependence on classified or "for elites only" type information is one of the things that has blinded our officials to economic and cultural realities in the last 40 years. Creative and well-modeled policy should be the driving force behind our economic and cultural doctrines, not the latest classified briefing on what we saw our enemy do or what China is doing that is countering our latest economic move. Watching and reacting to the tactical and operational moves of our enemies or economic competitors is a job for lieutenants, not senior statesmen and presidents. America's senior leadership needs to rise above a tactical or operational mindset and truly take strategic or universal stances that allow us to achieve greater things.

What I can say from connecting the attitudes of many of our leaders over the last two decades is that it isn't just the lieutenants that have the wrong attitudes driving bad decision making. *It's a lot of our nation's leadership.* I wish I could say different. Perhaps this is why President Trump fires so many of his senior leadership in search of better options. Don't get me wrong on American leaders. I've met some very wise and intelligent generals, CEO's and politicians. However, very logical strategic leaders are now a rarity. I can state that from thousands of firsthand accounts. I've interacted and listened to several generals, CEO's, and politicians who speak their philosophies concerning politics and economics. Most of them held a vast amount of knowledge. Much of it they seemingly believed was very strategic in nature. Unfortunately, most of what they said and how they thought was only tactical to operational in nature.

This book focuses on our leadership making better choices concerning economic, military, and cultural decisions. Our legislatures, our courts, and our executive leadership have gone politically shallow. I mean this in the most holistic sense of the word "shallow." It's not just that the bickering is more visible due to our high-tech social media society. Beginning with the baby-boomer generation, our leadership, despite what a particular senator or general may say, has been indoctrinated in our post-World-War II loyalty equals success so don't rock the boat doctrine.

Who could blame them for carrying on the tradition of seeing things economically as their parents saw things? After all, their parents succeeded in World War II and were the ones that supplied the world with raw materials and technology for 30 years after the war ended. Economics happened during this era the way they had to happen. It was volume that mattered, and businesses pushed products on dependent countries that were just happy to get them. Back then, America was the breadbasket of the world. Manufacturing efficiencies and business innovation didn't need to move very quickly. Because of that, we have become complacent. Older generations of Americans are still using the experiences of the 1960's to try and guide us back to a previous golden era of commerce that will never again be achievable due to the global changes that have occurred in economics.

We must create a different type of golden era for today's commerce. We must be better today than we were back then because our competition is better. Totally different economic strategies are needed in a world of fierce economic competition, a world where there is an intense need to measure and model business decisions in order to get it right. And, it's not just about the use of technology either. We have to create leaner, faster, and smarter processes all together than the previous golden era. When the golden era of commerce after World War II ran out, we didn't *measure, model, or invest well.*

Instead, we attempted to set up a domestic and global system through which to maintain the status quo of the post-World War II economic order. We are now beginning to feel the effects of the economic stressors that are the hidden drivers behind many of our current political and cultural conflicts. The price America is paying for our attitude and belief that we can "dominate through the old way of doing things" is only beginning to be felt. In that respect, in the last 40 years, our leadership has led us down a path that needs adjustment. We need to begin working together to create dynamic legislation and smarter investments for the benefit of all Americans. We owe it to our kids and grandkids to get this right.

In February of 2011, I was completing a Master's in Business Administration and looking for a job. I had mouths to feed so I was looking for work that could pay the bills while working whatever else I could manage. Life sucks when people are counting on you and you are letting them down. During the time between job applications, I began thinking about how messed up our current economy was and how it got into the situation in the first place. While I understood the buyer-beware component of capitalism, the unethical practices of the mortgage industry had definitely been allowed to get out-of-control. Our sales agents were simply cooking the mortgage application books and it was being allowed to happen on a large scale. What's more, our banking executives encouraged the unethical behavior, gave bonuses for the behavior, and even held classes to teach the behavior. In either case, bank executives who encouraged the behavior cashed out at the top and retired in luxury. The global economy nearly went bottom-up and would have without extensive intervention. A few years later, the wealthiest 1% of Americans had increased their wealth by thirty percent. It was the largest transfer of wealth from middle-class Americans to the ultra-wealthy in American history. Meanwhile, most Americans had to tighten their belts with many dipping into their retirement plans to make ends meet.

After doing some research on the reasons why political change is so difficult in America, I came to the conclusion at the time we probably should try and start a third political party because both Democrats and Republicans had fostered policies that essentially were promoting the same economics, often veiled as very different. I also felt we needed to move away from the existing political discourse. It had evolved into both sides demonizing each other, focusing on cultural issues while ignoring underlying economic realities. Currently, I don't know if a third party would help America or not. What I do know is that our current two-party system needs refinement in order to continue to be responsive to America's needs.

If that is not possible, a third political party creating disruption and change is the only alternative. Back in 2011, I didn't know much about Donald Trump. I knew he was a conservative businessman that was seemingly more open to cultural change. He had a habit of bucking convention which I thought could be a good thing given our current economic situation. So, I decided to write the page-and-a-half letter that follows. Please keep in mind my current beliefs about the American political system have changed since then. However, the letter has some content that I think is worth sharing in order to show that even an average guy like myself *can foresee* key elements of stress building within a political system and those stresses must be vented in order to prevent system collapse:

To whom it may concern (that may deliver this message to Donald Trump),

I respectfully request the contents within this letter be delivered or mentioned to Mr. Trump. I have attached my resume, references, and military separation document (DD-214) in order to verify my identity and background to ensure that this letter may be taken seriously.

Feb 25th, 2011

Mr. Trump,

     I am a 31-year old male former Marine Officer and aviator. I flew helicopters combat support missions in Iraq in 2005 and 2007. I was honorably discharged from the Marine Corps in 2009 of my own choosing because I wanted to pursue a civilian career and complete a graduate degree. I also consider myself a political scientist though I only have the rank of a BA in political science.

I introduced myself in order that you may consider an alternative in a possible run for the U.S. presidency. The last time a non-republican or democrat won the presidency was in 1850, when Millard Fillmore won as a Whig. The reasons for this are simple but misunderstood by most third party hopefuls, both candidates of modest means as well as wealthy candidates. The challenge of running as an independent or third party candidate is simply overcoming the lack of structure. It is hard to compete against political structures that have been in place for 160 years. However, both in Britain and the U.S. (both of which are primarily two-party systems), political parties do rise and fall. What has ALWAYS happened to facilitate this except in the cases of all out revolution (which I hope will not ever happen in the U.S.) is what I call "top-down-enablement." Bottom line, men and women of means have facilitated it by helping the average voter become a member of a new party rapidly. With the proper use of technology, the time to do this is now.

Most Americans identify themselves as moderates. There are even a number of websites up now devoted to the creation of "The American Moderate Party." I myself even reserved a website a few years back "usmoderate.com" but after studying the plight of creating a third party, realized it would take more than my efforts to create what is needed. Americans across the board wish they had another option, a party based off sound business principles and respect for modern concepts of freedom. I myself do not wish to run for office. I would like to help build a third party or be a political advisor.

Charlie Christ ran for U.S. Senate out of Florida in 2010. After having been a governor and knowing folks down there, he lost only by a handful of votes. I offered his campaign manager, his sister, my services. She was a fabulous person and we both enjoyed talking to each other. However, her campaign foreman simply did not know how to fight political maneuver warfare. I gave her foreman my resume and offered to speak at VA organizations throughout the state. However, I wasn't even used because my resume likely got lost is a pile of folders overwhelming the foreman. The campaign center was also run administratively not operationally. Charlie lost because he chose to run a campaign as a moderate instead of building a party and platform as a moderate. It does take a party. It takes a smart team to build a party too! It all can be done.

There is a website http://www.americanmoderateparty.org/ that gives a descent platform by which a third party candidate running as a moderate could delineate themselves from other candidates. However, this website falls horribly short of what is needed. It also has an older man (presumably the founder), that lectures his way through the differences between Republicans, Moderates, and Democrats. He's doing the best he can, but his website obviously falls far short of what is needed to attract attention and action. People want pictures and technology at their fingertips now-a-days. It's how things have become. Moderate candidates are making the same mistakes. They fall horribly short on building structure and enabling devices that would give the average voter the tools necessary to create local and state parties for exponential party growth.

I feel I understand what is necessary. The average voter needs a powerful registry to find a local party or club or the example templates to create a party at the local and state level rapidly. It can be done with legal structured templates integrated into an information resource center (a website that has teeth). Beyond this, recruitment of voters to the party (marketing) is essential. No other person I know is better situated as an American citizen to do this than you Mr. Trump.

A third party will eventually take the reins in the United States. Most candidates would never consider a run outside the comfort of the two major parties. If there ever is a time to do so, now is the time. The proper use of technology, (a facebook-like party website) coupled with the proper party structure and leadership, could grow rapidly at the state and local levels.

I have my thoughts on how to do this right. In either case, it takes a team. I offer my time and service to you if you believe this may be an option you would like to look into. ███████████████████

███████████████████████████████████

I am free to talk in person with anyone or just to talk over the phone. It would be an honor to work for you or simply to offer you my thoughts regarding this option.

Thank you for your time,

Sincerely,

████████████████

I never learned if now-President Trump ever received this letter. For all I know one of his lawyers or staff received it, maybe mentioned it, or maybe not. In the years that followed, I chose not to write about it because it didn't seem to matter. President Trump had considered a run for the presidency before and I'm one of the many folks that likely asked him to run. My advice described what Americans wanted: a President that could think for himself and affect change, independent of the two political parties that have controlled the direction of our country since before the American Civil War.

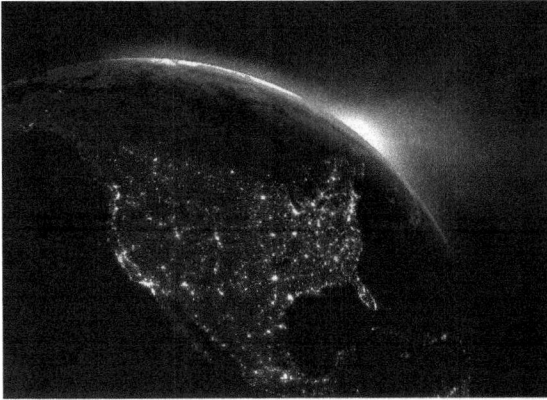

Chapter 2

America's Political Struggle Abbreviated

The two-party political system has its origins in western democratic nations. While one political party is in power, the other is out of power. The idea is simple yet profound. The out-of-power political party will keep tabs on elected officials in-power and make sure they are held accountable to the people. And, if things get too bad economically or socially, the other political party is an option for the people to vote the in-power political party out of office. The only problem with this setup is: what if both political parties know that their political structure will always be there? No matter what, the two political parties are the only option for the people if the other party upsets them too much.

The two political parties that have been in power for over 165 years realized this early on in their histories in America. Therefore, they have been mostly civil towards each other as they understood their shared interest in continued existence. The game was and still currently is, "Make the other political party seem as awful as possible," and "The people only have one other option to turn to for change." This wasn't always the case. Prior to the American Civil War, the long lifespan of a political party was no guarantee.

In either case, the stability of having two political parties has brought a lot of good to the American people in the last 165 years. It gave the people an outlet for change without revolution. While younger generations tend to look back on American history and see the tremendous amount of evil that has been facilitated through American politics (there indeed has been a lot of it), they tend to forget the stability having two stable political parties has brought. Yes, our American nation has preyed on native tribes as well as other societies that were weaker militarily than ourselves. In a lot of folks' opinions, we still do this regularly today. They'd say the Scandinavians taught the British, and the British taught the Americans how to win, not through fair competition but through war. They would also say Machiavellian tricks are what made Britain and America wealthy.

I'd have to disagree somewhat. While there were plenty of wars and dirty tricks to go around in the late medieval era leading up to Britain's dominance, war and dirty tricks were plentiful throughout the nations of Europe, America, and elsewhere. So, the utilization of these tactics became almost necessary for survival. This is not to minimize or whitewash the atrocities that occurred by no means. Britain played this terrible game well, was isolated from a lot of the ground fighting because of the English Channel, built a mighty navy to defend from invasion, and also was facilitated in its growth due to the culture of its people. Yes, Britain historically is one of the greatest enslavers of tribes and nations around the world for its own benefit. Its footprint of imperial influence actually dwarfs that of other nations including America if you accurately depict it. Even so, we cannot judge the Britain of the past or the America of the past. We must judge them on today's policies and character of their people. And today, there is no doubt that a great majority of British and American people are of good character and want to live peacefully in the world with other nations.

Looking back at the past, we have to remember most the nations of Europe as well as other strong nations around the world participated in terrible behavior to promote their economic growth. We cannot judge them on today's understanding of right or wrong. Ultimately, the people of Britain by and large respected the rule of law and the Crown's authority over them. This led to long-term civility. This is a key factor that promoted economic growth which many times we like to overlook in favor of pointing toward Britain's imperial methods, which like I said, were common at the time. Likewise, America grew to its current economic might primarily due to its' political structure and the culture of its' people.

Although there were major wars throughout America's history including the bloody American Civil War, we tend to forget that most of America's history was peaceful. America's expansion west across the American frontier and the ensuing conflict of the Native American people is another blemish on American expansion. I will not minimize the impact of this era on Native American tribes. What I will say again is that we cannot judge today's America from the actions of the America of the past.

Many other factors promoted America's growth in the last 250 years such as being isolated from the warring nations of Europe and having plentiful natural resources. However, political structure and a societal culture that respected governmental rule were key, or America would not be the superpower it is today. Throughout American history, our people utilized our political system to seek change. Having two stable political parties over a long period of time ensured that there was always one party with enough congressional votes to carry on the business of our nation. This was an effective way to help prevent constant gridlock within our House of Representatives, which is supposed to represent the American people.

Most of the Founding Fathers did not believe pure democracy was a good idea. They were right in that dictators have commonly gained power by stirring up the people and creating rebellion, often in ways destructive to society and not ending in more freedom. Many of the founders wanted the states to have equal representation, discounting a particular state's population altogether. Other Founders felt that this was a recipe for tyranny because with only a handful of men controlling state affairs, they might as well be under the rule of a King. So, these Founders wanted representation to be based on a state's population.

Ultimately, the Founders established both an upper and lower legislative house which was a good compromise. However, one must remember the fact that both houses represent the people and make the laws. The people do not directly make the laws on their own. Ultimately, the Senate became a second-tier buffer between the will of the people and actual change. The idea was to slow the cycle of discontent and allow change to occur slowly rather than rapidly through physical conflict. And, we had our courts of course that through the wise choice of the Bill-of-Rights, has always been supposed to ensure our rights as individuals against the evils of overbearing government or other unjust citizens (That's why Justice is Blindfolded). For most of our history, this structure has served us well despite the many ills associated with specific generations violating the rights of different groups of people such as minorities, women, and LGTBQ Americans. We still struggle with this cultural conflict today but have evolved greatly since our early days as a nation. That's the American political system in a nutshell.

So, why are the last few decades any different than previous years politically or economically? How can we say we need a different type of change now? The primary question is, "Is it possible that our political system has evolved incorrectly in the last

40 years setting us up for failure? Or, is where we are today the result of what is supposed to have happened, a design from the *will of the people* appropriately buffered and guided by the hands of the Senate and our Supreme Court? If we have evolved somehow incorrectly in the last 40 years, what is it that has gone wrong?

What we do know is that our current political system has its hands tied by a literal embedding of special interests groups that are now required for its own survival. It takes massive amounts of money to get elected to Congress and especially to the U.S. Senate within almost every U.S. district now. If you don't get the pass from deep pockets, you most likely don't get the pass to run as the front runner on either political party's ticket. There's a price to be paid to get to run. That price is allowing special interest legislation to pass through both houses of Congress unimpeded. Is it any wonder then why for the last 40 years, our legislatures have consistently created massive spending waste? None of this spending has benefited Americans with a better wage, a better education, better infrastructure, or safer retirement incomes. Of this monetary waste, even if one-fourth of it had been invested in Americans in a sensible way, we would have transformed America into a better place to live and work in the last 40 years. We could have expected a better future.

How dare current politicians such as Nancy Pelosi and Joe Biden who've had careers creating wasteful legislation stand up as of late and say they want a better life for lower-income Americans. Politicians such as Joe Biden and Nancy Pelosi, as well as most other Congressional or Senatorial leaders to include Republicans such as Senate majority-leader Mitch McConnell, have sold Americans down the drain to secure their own careers. This is why we are where we are now, a country that cannot afford to keep up with Western standards of living to include health care, education, infrastructure, and social security. Do I blame a specific congressional leader? No. I mention former Vice President Joe

Biden, our current Speaker-of-the-House Nancy Pelosi, and Senator Mitch McConnell only to show that even the most well-meaning of politicians are not getting the job done when it comes to helping lower-income and middle-class Americans create a better life. The system required specific behaviors of these politicians and they obliged; otherwise, they would not have had long careers in Washington D.C at all. All Americans have a responsibility to help change this system that now owns the votes of our representatives and senators.

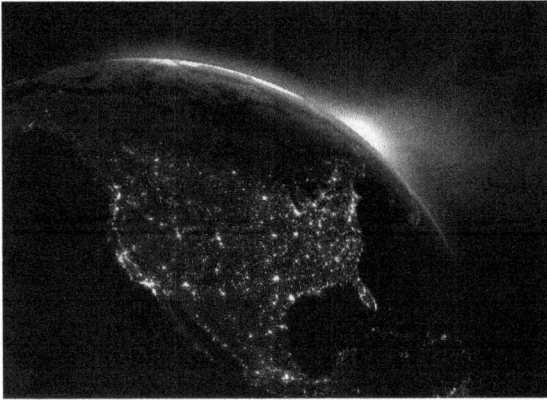

PART II

Facilitating Better Economics

"The King will reply, 'Truly I tell you, whatever you did for one of the least of these brothers and sisters of mine, you did for me."

-Jesus Christ describing the scene of the Final Judgement

(The Bible-New International Version, Matthew 25:40)

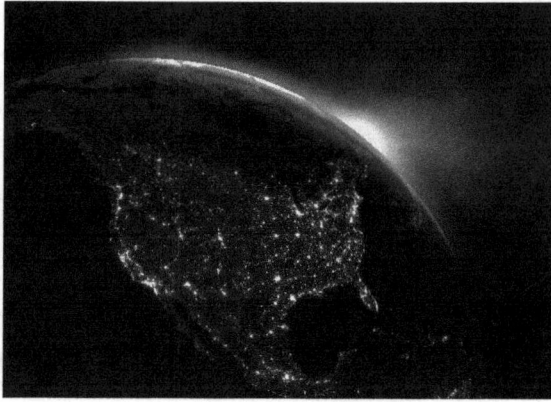

Chapter 3

Beyond Economics 101:

Climbing to a Higher Income Bracket

American Incomes 1999-2017

The U.S. Census Bureau most often represents its income findings by using a number called a median (it shows the middle income based on the number of Americans instead of the average). A median better represents an overall population's middle. That said, we will use the median income and look at incomes from 1999 to 2017 to see what we get:

Median American Income 1999-2017

(Inflation Adjusted to 2017 Dollars)

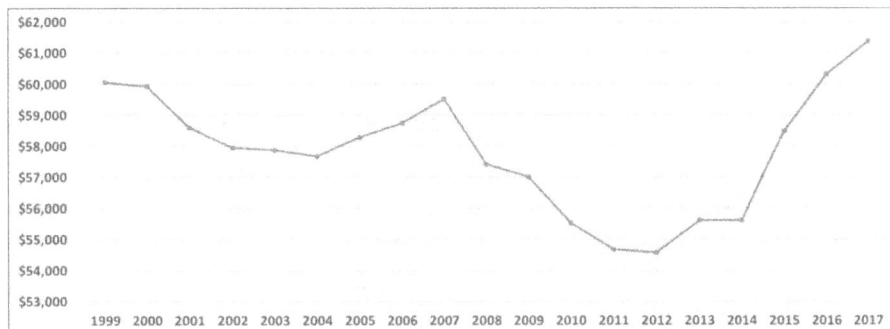

Over a period of 18 years, the graph above seems to say most Americans ended up about where they started before the 2001 dot-com bubble burst and the 2008 financial crisis. While that may be true, it doesn't show which Americans suffered the most and which Americans suffered little or even prospered. To see this, we need to bracket American incomes:

American Household Incomes 1999-2017

(Inflation Adjusted to 2017 Dollars):

Income Dispersion Percentile	1999	2017	Difference in Annual Pay
10th percentile limit	$15,269	$14,219	-6.9%
20th percentile limit	$25,291	$24,638	-2.6%
40th percentile limit	$47,110	$47,110	0.0%
50th (median)	$60,062	$61,372	2.2%
60th percentile limit	$74,361	$77,552	4.3%
80th percentile limit	$116,937	$126,855	8.5%
90th percentile limit	$159,067	$179,077	12.6%
95th percentile limit	$209,575	$237,034	13.1%

It is evident that about half of American households stayed within income brackets that were declining or growing very slowly from 1999 through 2017. This is even with the huge run-up in stock market prices from 2011 through 2017. During the period, half of Americans really couldn't take advantage of the boom due to their lower real wages. In the long run, it does an individual or family no good if they cannot save any of their money to have a better standard of living in the future. *This is part of the reason why President Trump was elected.* Lower-income and middle-class Americans wanted to try something new. Electing anyone outside of the normal political system, even an unconventional businessman like candidate Trump, was a far better prospect for them than electing an insider like former First Lady Hillary Clinton.

Besides the income and wealth inequities previously seen, the gap between male and female pay as well as the gap between whites and minority incomes have not improved greatly and continue to be huge issues. Our federal agencies also track these numbers and are aware. I lack the book length to get into all of that, but those inequities are very important to consider in addition to income brackets. President Obama had eight years in office to try and help resolve these inequities.

By the end of his presidency, things were shifting for the better but were not really fast enough to make a difference. He missed a golden opportunity to help half of Americans just like all the other presidents since Reagan missed the same opportunity. President Obama's administration, like previous administrations, simply didn't know how to transition away from "Reaganomics." The rich had gotten a lot richer under President Obama's watch but the poor and middle-class, unlike his promise, did not achieve any significant improvement in their overall living standards.

This is the same issue facing president Trump today leading up to the 2020 election. President Trump has made some strides helping lower-income and middle-income Americans' wages.

However, the gains are still too slow. The question for many Americans is, what could President Trump do about it with a second term? Many lower-income Americans have a gut instinct that although President Trump does cater to the rich and powerful like all Presidents have, they believe once reelected for a second term he is likely to take some policies he has control over into his own hands. They believe that he, more than any other insider, is more likely to help Americans stuck on the bottom and in the middle raise their standards of living.

What is for certain is that the latest proposal by Nancy Pelosi, our Speaker of the House, for a stair-stepped increase in our minimum wage is not what it seems. Per the campaign words of previous Vice President, Joe Biden (when speaking to wealthy Americans), "no one's standard of living will change, nothing would fundamentally change" if he's elected President. He made this explicitly clear. This is a clear message to America's established wealthy that Joe Biden would work for them. Nancy Pelosi's published dates for minimum wage increases will allow our federally controlled banks to know exactly when to manipulate inflation to match any wage increase lower-income Americans get. Nancy is simply asking for a reset of the Reaganomics timeline where the cycle can start all over again. So, "nothing would fundamentally change" is absolutely correct if Joe Biden were elected as President of the United States and executed Nancy Pelosi's plan. Americans of lower-income brackets could get a temporary income boost then each pay raise tier would be eaten up with inflation manipulation within months. The Reagan Doctrine of economics would be maintained utilizing the labor of lower 50% of Americans to create wealth for the top 5%. Reagan's doctrine has by no means been a "trickle down" economics doctrine in the last 40 years. Contrary to popular opinion, beginning with Reagan in 1981 until today, wealth has "trickled up" from lower-income and middle-class Americans:

Share of Income Distribution 1980-2016

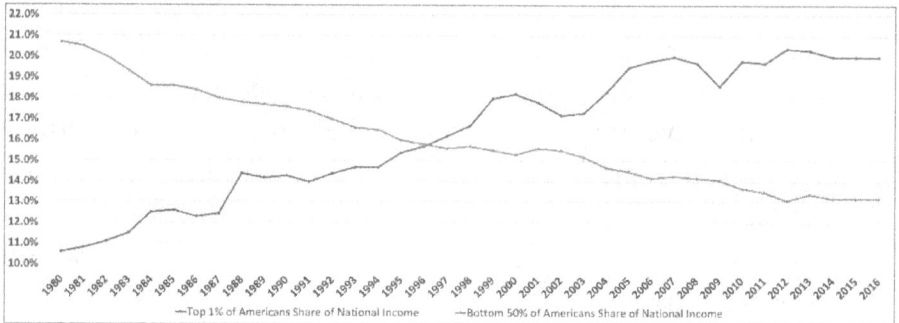

Chart legend: —Top 1% of Americans Share of National Income   —Bottom 50% of Americans Share of National Income

During the Reagan Era, the minimum wage decreased the most within the last 40 years and has never recovered. It is a fact that America's lower-income and lower middle-income Americans got poorer under President Reagan and have never recovered since. As part of a plan to curb inflation and encourage business growth, minimum wage became more controlled under Reagan by the mere fact that it was not increased as the cost of living increased:

Real Minimum Wage 1956-2018

(Inflation Adjusted to 2018 Dollars)

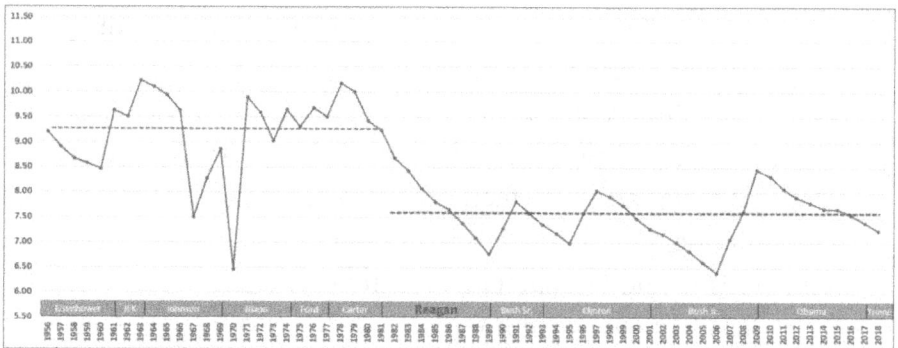

Contrary to what Reagan preached against, Reagan's action of not increasing the minimum wage had the effect of controlling the minimum wage just as commodity prices are controlled in socialist regimes. "Reaganomics" desynched minimum wage policies from attempting to provide low-income Americans with an acceptable cost of living. Instead, it controlled low-income human labor like a commodity price. We have done this since "Reaganomics" began in the early 1980's. Presidents G.H.W. Bush, Clinton, G.W. Bush, Obama, and even Trump have all carried on this economic doctrine. President Obama claimed differently by preaching "Middle Class" economics. Unfortunately, his policies showed a strict adherence to Reagan Doctrine.

To put it bluntly, Reagan's economic methods are stolen right out of the playbook of pretty hardcore socialist regimes. These types of economic control techniques are used in communist countries where the lowest income bracket's labor is controlled like a commodity as an input to the overall economy. The primary goal of these techniques is to ensure production output rather than attempting to ensure the lower-income bracket has a reasonable living wage. The idea is, "let the lower-income bracket hurt as much as possible prior to raising the wage." Rather than "not controlling" minimum wage like Reagan was seemingly able to convince most of America's elites and middle-class of, controlling minimum wage was exactly what Reagan did. Reagan was in fact a great fixer of the minimum wage. His method of *not allowing it to rise* helped keep inflation under control and true labor costs ever declining where businesses could grow.

Keeping minimum wage suppressed can only go on so long if inflation is occurring causing the cost of food staples to rise. Americans on the bottom have to eat. Unlike what has been stated by politicians as an excuse for suppressing it, it's not just school kids and part-time workers depending on the minimum wage. Families depend on it.

Reaganomics is clever. Without suppressing minimum wage as long as possible though, it doesn't work. Why do you think long term Republican Senator Mitch McConnell is so against raising the minimum wage? *He knows it has tremendous effect. The minimum wage also has a marked effect on entry-level technical and salary job wages as well. It is a marker that other workers compare their relative wages against.* I would suggest to the Senator that even if we held off raising the minimum wage for now, it would *have to be raised* shortly after President Trump is reelected to sustain any economic growth whatsoever otherwise spending for a whole half of Americans would collapse putting us into a deep recession:

Real Minimum Wage 1956-2018

(Inflation Adjusted to 2018 Dollars)

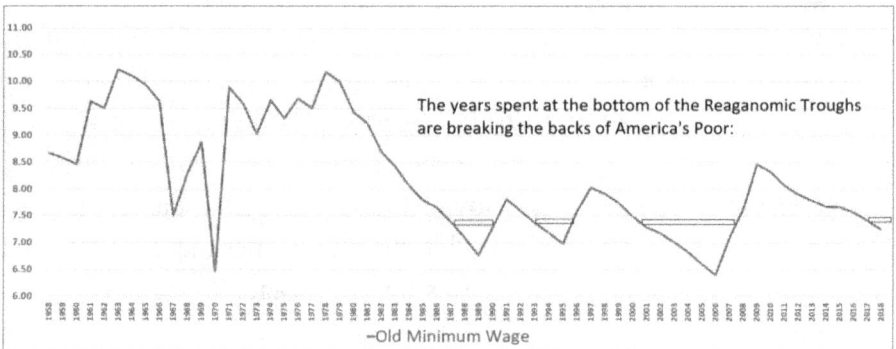

The years spent at the bottom of the Reaganomic Troughs are breaking the backs of America's Poor:

—Old Minimum Wage

If I ever spoke to the Senator, I would tell him:

"Senator, we are nearing the bottom of the Reaganomics cycle (far right of the graph above). Letting the Democrats take this issue from the President likely wasn't a smart play on your part because it wasn't in the best interest of President Trump. I would think you have a special responsibility to the President and your political party to come across as knowledgeable and considerate of the plight of America's poor. As of late Senator, you seem to be coming off as of having no concern for a lot of low-income and middle-class voters who depend on the minimum wage. You also seem to try to show you are managing the President's economics for him to some extent. I would say the President of the

27

United States has the right to make up his own mind concerning what he thinks about the minimum wage and that both hands of the Senate should respect that. He can then take his beliefs to Congress and ask for legislation on behalf of the American people that can fix the current broken system Reagan's administration established and both political parties have reinforced in the last 40 years. If President Trump feels taking the reins away from the Democrats on this issue is a good thing, he has the right to do that. He also has the right to look at totally new options concerning managing the minimum wage. I would also encourage you to look at other options with the President for actually making the minimum wage work on a sustainable basis. While you are right in the fact that we cyclically over adjust the minimum wage to the high side, we also under adjust it letting inflation degrade its buying power. Both Democrats and Republicans are managing the minimum wage incorrectly. You either want to stop the bleeding that Reaganomics causes among low-income Americans, or you don't. If you don't, you're in the same boat as Democrats. And, for the last 40 years, both hands of the Senate have been in this boat together."

I would say this even while *I am not for simply raising the minimum wage like Nancy Pelosi and Joe Biden are asking. This would restart another Reaganomic Economic Cycle creating massive inflation that the government uses as a cheap loan.* Both Democrats and Republicans have become dependent on this cycle. Instead, a smarter move for America is to formulize the minimum wage, making American economics stronger. We are a great country. We can do better than argue every few years about the same rudimentary issues. Let's do a little Algebra and get this right for Americans. Let's depoliticize the minimum wage and propel America into stronger economics. It is unbecoming of our political elite to dumb down how things actually work in order to seek favor of the system that rewards them. All brethren and sisters of our political system have a responsibility to seek greater wisdom in how we manage our economics. It's departing from what our Founders intended if we do not. Seek strength and betterment of your fellow human beings or step aside so others more willing to stand for their fellow Americans can make America a better place to live and work.

One of the core methods of Reaganites is spending large amounts of government tax money on government programs that do not invest heavily back into the middle-income and lower-income classes. They do this while at the same time suppressing wages. This is because production under the largest corporations is easier to ramp up than growing American community businesses. This action of funneling production to large businesses has begun to strain small American communities to the breaking point. The average American now has to travel to larger communities to find a decent job. Whatever small business growth statistics Republicans like to flaunt concerning the last few years of small business growth are flawed in the sense that the statistics are fragile. What they will not tell you is that these small businesses are the ones that take the brunt of economic downturns. Many of them go out of business during the downturns because of the Reaganomics setup. While some large businesses struggle, a higher proportion of them survive during economic downturns. Thus, a purging cycle that pits large corporations against small businesses is created. During recessions, it is the large businesses who get the bulk share of government spending and enjoy that cushion to fall back on. Small businesses on average are left to fend for themselves. Because Reaganomics promotes deeper recessions, small businesses are baited during the good times to spend then during recessions are quickly switched to financial failure when their cash flows do not support their ongoing credit balances. It is then that their commercial assets are bought up by corporations or the ultra-wealthy. This is the purging cycle Reaganomics promotes. This setup is rigged to funnel ongoing production and wealth to the top.

Reaganites are beyond convincing that what they are doing is very bad for the country's long-term health. Each time the market crashes hard and the poor and middle-classes show ever increasing inabilities to cope, they blame it on America not being even more Reagan-like. This reaction is socialist to the core when it comes to government management of the business cycle. It has taken a few decades, but it is showing up in a big way. American economics has pretty much become like an athlete on steroids. Muscle mass is built until the athlete gets sick and collapses and must take an extended leave of absence to recover. This happened in 1987, 2001, and 2008 and could occur again soon. While these stock market and economic slowdowns had other contributing root causes, all of them happened when America's poor was beneath a living wage:

<u>Minimum Wage's connection to Economic Collapses 1980-2016</u>

(Inflation Adjusted to 2018 Dollars)

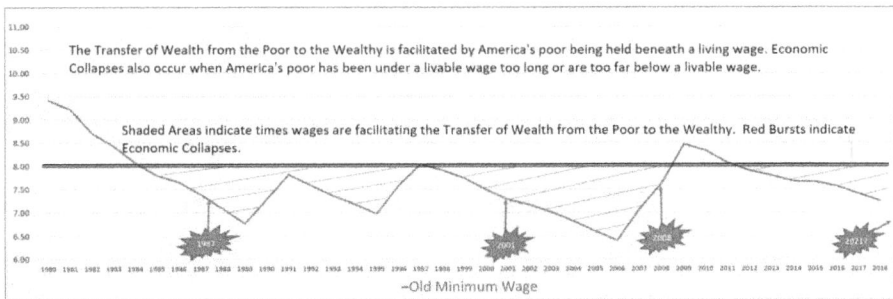

The Transfer of Wealth from the Poor to the Wealthy is facilitated by America's poor being held beneath a living wage. Economic Collapses also occur when America's poor has been under a livable wage too long or are too far below a livable wage.

Shaded Areas indicate times wages are facilitating the Transfer of Wealth from the Poor to the Wealthy. Red Bursts indicate Economic Collapses.

—Old Minimum Wage

I wonder if Reagan was thinking about this when he began his policy of juicing the lower half of earners in America to make the top 50% happier (and the top 5% extremely happy). I doubt it. Small deviations below a working wage matters for the economy at large. That is why a smarter minimum wage facilitated through formulation would make things better and potentially stave off another economic collapse in 2021. As debt has increased for the United States, the lower 50% of Americans can no longer support increased growth to keep up with the debt ratio. Make no mistake about it, the lower 50% of American incomes are ultimately the foundation to American prosperity when all the government spending is exhausted.

In simple terms, we have become too top-heavy. The federal government's wasteful programs and lack of investment back into America's working classes has overweighed and unbalanced the ship. How could our country promote policies in the last 40 years that have literally bled the bottom 50% incomes of Americans and funnel it to the top? It's unethical and brutal. If you're making the top half of Americans happy, I suppose those are the Americans who are most affluent and matter to our government. So, "Who cares about the other 50%", is what an average elite might say.

I would ask our government to reconsider this course. It is anti-Judeo-Christian in all respects. This economic method, because of how it lacked and continues to lack established reinvestment thresholds to reinvest back into American communities, is obviously deeply flawed. The outputs of this economic method have come to a point that they are about to wreck the American way-of-life. I'd ask that our American Government and the higher-income brackets not push the tab for this failed economic method off onto our lower-income and middle-income Americans. They didn't get us into this mess. I'd ask our Government and higher-income bracket Americans to have the God-given decency as human beings of conscious to take responsibility for this mess and fix it. If Reagan were alive today and I could speak with him, I would say:

> "President Reagan, good idea but bad judgement in how you implemented your economic method. It's turned out to be bad juju for America."

Neither Democrats or Republican Presidents, Congressmen, or Senators have addressed this income inequality since the 1980's plunge where minimum wage no longer provided a life above poverty for low-income Americans. Our current financial banking system has essentially set up a response mechanism where the cost of living rises rapidly to meet any minimum wage increase. This keeps the federal minimum wage from ever returning to the pre-Reagan era level which averaged three dollars more an hour than the wages of the last 40 years (when inflation adjusted). Reagan was the turning point at which the American government no longer waited on the people to decide how the economy would go. With Reagan, America essentially became a semi-managed industrialized economy. While that may not be a bad thing at all, what is evident is, this period coincided with large gains for America's upper classes while America's lowest paid workers seemingly footed the bill.

I propose we depoliticize our federal minimum wage. Let it follow a refined set of rules to be evaluated at the end of each fiscal year and changed as necessary dependent on the economic situation. This is an all-around-safer way of managing minimum wage and will smooth out the bumps lower-income Americans feel over time. I believe it will help the overall economy manage wage growth and the sustainment of GDP as well:

Proposed Federal Minimum Wage Formula

KEY		The Higher of:
New Minimum Wage Should Be	A	$A = (1.4*C)/2080$
Previous Year's Minimum Wage	B	or
Individual Poverty Line Annual Income	C	$A = B$

How do we know this simple formulation works well? The answer is, we can do some mathematical modeling to see what would have happened if we would have used these formulas since 1958 instead of the rigid and reactive minimum wage hikes that occurred. A formulized minimum wage would have led to a healthier growth in our GDP as more money would have been invested across our communities throughout America instead of the top-heavy-system we have today that has not reinvested back into our communities. We know a smarter set of rules for minimum wage management would have smoothed the wrinkles out in our last six decades of economic cycles making it less painful for America's lower-income workers. The minimum wage will still lose value over the course of a year due to inflation. However, one year of wage lag is much better than six to eight years. The new proposed minimum wage would also help alleviate the tendency to over adjust the minimum wage to the high side after long periods of time with it going unadjusted:

Minimum Wage Since 1958 (Proposed Versus Old Method)

(Inflation Adjusted to 2018 Dollars at 140% 2018 Poverty Guideline)

—Old Minimum Wage   —Proposed Minimum Wage

The proposed formulized minimum wage as seen in the trend above, would have provided a more stable labor market for small businesses nationwide. The model above shows year-to-year as well as intra-year declines in the value of minimum wage due to inflation. Notice that even with this greater intra-year variation depicted, over a 60-year period, the proposed formularized minimum wage would have kept true minimum wage within $1.10 of optimum. It can be done. And, it will make American economics stronger. *I am not saying I have the perfect formula, just a decent one.* I am up for improving it as we all should be. If we can build nuclear ships and land on the moon, we can figure out a simple formula to make the American minimum wage work better.

It is very difficult for small businesses to hire and keep minimum wage labor at the bottom of a Reagan economic trough. The wage is simply too far below the cost of living at this point. Like I said previously, small deviations truly matter for people making our minimum wage. People simply stop working for minimum wage or depart as soon as they find a better job when minimum wage has dropped too far below 140% of the poverty guideline's hourly wage. Vacancies for these jobs then go unfilled just like is happening in today's labor market. At a critical point, this starts hurting the economy as a whole.

Contrary to what Reaganites would say, a minimum wage cycle with less squeeze on our poor will help businesses keep employees and grow the economy. President Reagan's method attempts to help businesses, but its process has proven to be too damaging to our nation's health to be sustainable. It has depleted the adaptable wealth of the bottom-half of American incomes and this creates deep recessions. The wealth of the bottom half of Americans has a stabilizing effect on the country.

The lack of refinement in President Reagan's method has hurt tens of millions of Americans and set us up for an unsustainable economic path. Over the course of the last 40 years, this economic squeeze cycle has hurt the long-term economic health of 50% of American incomes, the incomes that form the base of the American economy. If a smarter formulized system of managing minimum wage would have been in place over the last 40 years, we would not have had the violent business cycles draining foundational wealth from lower-income and middle-class Americans.

In conjunction with more stable wealth, we still could have had more wealth creation within the top 50% of income levels as well because we would not have had so deep of destructive business cycles we've experienced. A smarter formulized minimum wage will provide more stability for American families, individuals, and small businesses across the board, creating greater stability for the middle-classes.

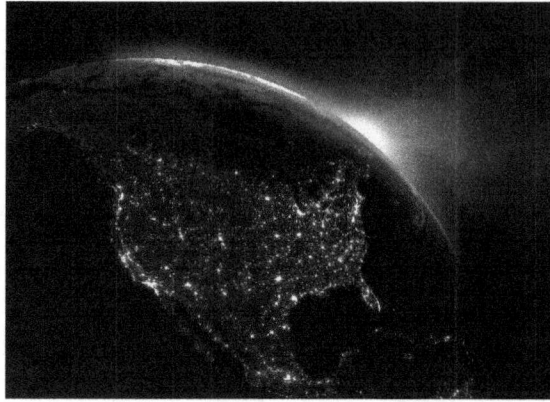

Chapter 4

The Budget, Deficits & Wasteful Spending

What we spend our citizens' money on matters. Money spent is like food eaten. While junk food can give you energy and help you pull an all-nighter, at some point your health begins to be negatively affected. This is what has happened to America in the last 40 years. We've invested terribly letting our education, infrastructure, and technology development programs fall behind many other Western nations. What is more alarming is that, *we've had the money to do better than most other Western nations*. Now that America's business growth opportunities have begun to decline because of our poor governmental investments, large companies have put their money in overseas accounts. This is a hoarding stage; these companies will buy up assets in America once the economy downturns and asset prices collapse. That's what they are waiting on right now. Not for America to prosper, but for America to fail where they can capture more wealth as they did between 2009 and 2012.

We cannot blame other countries such as China for being in this situation. Our own businesses and our government fostered this deep and painful cycle we have been going through for the last 40 years by not investing back into America with our tax dollars. How do we know? We know because of the junk we've spent our money on that has failed to raise our standard of living for half of Americans as well as failed to protect us from terrorism. At the same time, the wasteful spending increased American cultural tensions across the board. Our wasteful spending has funneled government tax dollars to the wealthy by spending about a quarter of all tax dollars on waste that supported ultra-wealthy businesses that did not add value to sustaining our long-term health as a nation. Both Democrats, Republicans, our judiciaries, as well as previous Presidents have created an ongoing governmental system that engages in theft of Americans' tax dollars, funneling them to ultra-wealthy business interests. Our society is greatly suffering today because of this behavior.

It is difficult to compare American federal budgets to each other from year-to-year. Departments change names or new departments are created every few years. Ultimately though, Americans still have the same basic need categories. What percentage of each fiscal year's budget we spend on those overall categories greatly matters. Hiding certain government spending behind administrative categories is a form of lying to the American people, one that has become the norm for most Presidents and legislative bodies.

Ultimately, we should require all budgets to be able to be compared to each other through a "What are we spending the Money on?" category system. On the next page is a generalized spending category list that divides all government spending up into eight spending categories. Standardizing this from year-to-year will allow our Presidents, Senators, and Congressional leaders to see the *big picture*. Beyond this, we should do the work to categories the previous 50 years' worth of American budgets into this same system. This will allow us to see where we are now relative to our previous history of investing back into America:

Seeing Where the Federal Budget is Going

Federal Spending Category	Includes*	Notes/Explanations
Infrastructure %	Examples include but are not limited to: All Roads, Bridges, Dams, Canals, Waterways Airports, and federal Public Works related Spending	Includes Retiree benefits of related Agencies.
Education %	Examples include but are not limited to: Any and all federal Spending on Education to include Scholarships and the GI Bill, and School Construction Assistance	The GI Bill is included in this and not *Keeping us Safe* Category because studies show that the contribution to education of our Troops creates economic benefits such as small business growth etc. Includes Retiree benefits of related Agencies.
Commerce %	Examples but not limited to: Energy, Agriculture, Labor	Services that make the nation stronger through development of Business or Commerce related Activities. Includes Retiree benefits of related Agencies.
Keeping Us Safe %	Examples include but are not limited to: All Military & Defense Spending, CIA, Homeland Security, Policing Agencies such as the FBI, NSA, DEA, U.S. Marshals, Border Patrol, Space Program, Advanced Research Agencies such as DARPA, federal Prisons, as well as Government, Military Retirees and Veteran Pension Benefits & Hospitals	The Space Program is included in the *Keeping us Safe* category because much of the Science of the Space Program began in the military such as X-Planes and advanced Rocketry. When comparing across decades before NASA was in existence, it is important to keep it in the same bucket. While the Space program gives us other benefits besides *Keeping us Safe*, it has contributed greatly to military technology as far as spy satellites and missile technology currently on the cutting edge of military tactics. Therefore, it is best tracked under this category over long periods to be comparable to previous decades. All Veteran related expenses besides the GI Bill are the cost of doing business for the U.S. Military and it is fiscally delusional to not see them as such. Also Includes Retiree benefits of related Agencies.
Health & Human Services, and Interior Services %	Examples include but are not limited to: FDA, OSHA, National Parks, federal Vaccination, Health Services, Gov Healthcare, Research Facilities, Medicaid and Other Dept Interior Spending	Services that make our lives better by preventing disease, protecting the environment, promoting healthier living, providing healthcare, maintaining National Parks, or other programs that improve our health or our lives but do not necessarily protect us from foreign invasion or prevent terrorism. Includes Retiree benefits of related Agencies.
Social Security & Financial Welfare %	Examples include but are not limited to: Social Security, Earned-Income Credits, Food Assistance	All Monetary Payments to Citizens other than Veteran Benefits Includes Retiree benefits of related Agencies.
Paying Down the Debt %	All monetary transactions or losses due to federal debt management	Includes Retiree benefits of related Agencies.
All Other %	All other Budget Spending not included in above Categories	Includes Retiree benefits of related Agencies.

*Any state or Local Grant Money should also be divided into the above functional categories as a way of seeing what we are spending our money on percentagewise.

If split up like this, I imagine Presidents, Senators, Congressional leaders, and our bureaucrats would see a different picture than what they commonly see and report. I would think the *Keeping us Safe* Category would be twice the size or more each year than what is reported simply as Defense Spending. If we spent more wisely in the *Keeping Us Safe* category, we could easily spend more in the *Infrastructure, Education and Commerce* categories which would promote long-term health and growth for America in the future. I believe we can do a much better job at keeping Americans safe while at the same time, spending less.

Large businesses that benefit from all the Defense contracts would not be happy and that could affect what they'd give to election campaigns. But, if that's the right thing to do, that's the right thing to do. Presidents and congressional leaders must start taking responsibility for investing in key components of our nation's long-term health. Those components can be mathematically modeled in order to establish key threshold minimums as a percentage of GDP to foster nominal growth. Our congressional leaders should hold themselves accountable to those thresholds no matter their political affiliation.

When nations invest wisely, they learn they do not need massive amounts of heavy machinery that are technologically obsolete in 20 years in order to keep them safe. As far as actually keeping American safe, one strong military analyst with excellent foreign language skills trained with the tenacity to win can be worth more than a whole squadron of joint-strike-fighters. That's a fact. We learned that lesson 18 years ago. Considering the cost of maintenance and all the other personnel paychecks, that one military analyst and associated handlers cost 1,000 times less than a squadron of joint-strike-fighters (JSF) (three million dollars versus three billion dollars). Yes of course we need our military hardware too; but again, a squadron of joint-strike-fighters or battalion of tanks isn't going to stop the next massive cyber-attack on America or figure out a terrorist is planning to detonate a dirty bomb in one of America's largest cities.

Smart networks of people working with the latest lean technology do those things. Those networks of people and applicable enabling technology are less expensive than buying heavy pieces of military machinery that in today's battlefield, are not what they used to be. Anything that is not hyper-sonic in the next 30 years including joint-strike fighters are basically going to be "policing grade" military technology, not cutting-edge battlefield technology.

Congress, Americans would request of you to stop buying too many units of machines from programs such as this that look good but are not what they seem. When programs take 20 years to get concepts operational, they are near obsolete by the time they are fielded due to rapidly changing technology and tactics. True break throughs in technology change the game rather than just make something look cooler and fly a bit faster or with more range. Sometimes, breakthroughs are much cheaper than previous technology. If they are not, you have to question if the program is financially sustainable. Many cheaper defensive weapons can totally negate the need for higher costing offensive weapons as well.

The Joint Strike Fighter is a good example of a high cost defense program where its technology is already becoming obsolete compared to hypersonic missile technology. We've been developing the JSF for nearly 30 years. It's technology is old. We should think long and hard before we commit our nation to buying into another large defense program like the JSF program that ultimately could let us down. Technology moves too fast for that and we knew better than to do this (I will discuss more on technological dominance in *The Pursuit of Technology* chapter). We should think calm and collectively rather than being intimidated by corporate defense contractors and military brass who will come in hard with a sales pitch concerning just how dominating their technology is. They just want to spend, and their existence depends on spending. They should only be advisors to demonstrate asset capabilities not the ultimate decision makers when it comes to spending.

I know it sounds like it, but I didn't mean to beat up on the JSF program. *There is a bigger picture here.* For the control of most skies in the next 30 years, the JSF will be great. Most militaries will not have near-space or upper atmosphere hypersonic missiles in the next 30 years. For the ones that will, we will not be going to war with anyways unless we plan to start a nuclear war; which, I do not believe is on the Pentagon's agenda. (There is one exception, Iran, which I will discuss in the *National Security Policy* chapter). In either case, this particular discussion is about governmental spending. There is no doubt we can be smarter with our *Keeping Us Safe* spending at home and abroad.

As congressional leaders, doing the right thing may mean you will need to limit future spending or even kill a program that costs a massive amount of money. This may be the case even though this program *could economically benefit your congressional district*. Is it the right thing to do for our country as a whole, or just the right thing to bring your congressional district more jobs? Those are not always the same things despite what you might think. Once military spending starts in one area folks want to keep it started no matter what and they fight tooth and nail to keep it going. That increases the country's overhead semi-permanently. Over time, it bleeds the country dry with a lot of waste in overall spending. This is spending that could have been spent on leaner and smarter programs that actually could have made America safer. A program's utility must be decided in a political venue isolated from the "who gets the money" portion of the decision making.

Have a sense of honor to our nation's flag over getting reelected. That's the job of congressional leadership. Have loyalty to our people and our nation's flag above getting to say you brought

2000 defense spending jobs to your district. If our country truly has a higher priority and you do not do your due diligence to find that higher priority for where our money should have been spent, you're wasting our tax dollars and taking the easy route. You're playing politics rather than protecting Americans. You truly are selling our country's future down the drain to help promote your career. This is partly the reason why we are in the situation we are in now in America, trillions and trillions of wasted tax dollars, with no ROI for Americans. Congressmen must stop letting defense companies and military brass sell them stuff that costs us trillions without a true ROI of making America safer!

Nations learn that forgetting about their infrastructure, education, commerce, and safety net social programs in favor of cutting taxes on the ultra-wealthy will one day catch up with them as the ultra-wealthy are not financing our roads, bridges, schools, or defense programs. It is failed logic to believe that so long as GDP grows, we create more tax dollars to be able to invest back into America and things will be ok. That only works if ongoing investments back into America have occurred over decades. Certain lack of investments over time, *we don't get back*. You cannot fully make up for the lack of educating a child properly when they are an adult. That leaves a permanent mark that only a huge amount of personal fortitude can overcome.

You cannot make up for a lack of investment into the space program over 40 years when other nations begin to catch up to us and we lose the benefit the space program has provided us concerning the development of a broad range of technologies for 60 years. You cannot make up for a mother who had to work for 20 years while raising three kids instead of staying home like she wanted to in order to focus on her kids' development. She and her spouse both had to work to make ends meet due to sky-rocketing healthcare and education costs combined with the deteriorating value of minimum wage. Government taxes are supposed to

42

reinvest back into society on an ongoing basis in a wise and strategic manner. Because of the element of time, as a nation, somethings we don't get back the things we lose because of poor investments.

Large corporations see what is happening since they have been given the greatest share of government spending in the last 40 years. They've become ultra-wealthy with large cash reserves with many of those reserves in overseas accounts avoiding American taxation. They currently see the tide turning and know Americans have had enough of the pain they've experienced for the last 40 years. We're simply not standing right by them and even some wealthy members of society are recognizing this. Consider the following that was recently (2019) put out by the Business Roundtable, an organization with input from many of America's largest corporations concerning business ethics:

> FROM CNBC: The reimagined idea of a corporation drops the age-old notion that corporations function first and foremost to serve their shareholders and maximize profits. Rather, investing in employees, delivering value to customers, dealing ethically with suppliers and supporting outside communities are now at the forefront of American business goals, according to the statement.

> FROM THE ROUNDTABLE: "While each of our individual companies serves its own corporate purpose, we share a fundamental commitment to all of our stakeholders," said the statement signed by 181 CEOs. "We commit to deliver value to all of them, for the future success of our companies, our communities and our country."

> "The American dream is alive, but fraying," Jamie Dimon, chairman and CEO of J.P. Morgan Chase and chairman of Business Roundtable, said in a press release.

I don't think very wealthy people sit up at the top and think, "How can we make life more miserable for the average American today?" I don't think that's how it works. That being said, it is obvious our economic system has greatly rewarded our CEO's, other leaders and wealth holders of our society in the last 40 years. It seems that they should be able to reflect on this failed economic system and figure out how they could contribute to making things better for the 50% of Americans left behind. It seems our government has not taken the leadership on this effort. Maybe we should consider letting business leaders if they actually care get more involved. Something tells me about half of Americans don't fully trust these business leaders; but, to really change things for the better, these folks will have to get involved anyways. So, why not ask them to get more involved? It's the right thing to do.

Besides promoting community strength through corporate charity foundations, corporate leaders and other wealthy individuals could challenge themselves to take direct action as well. This would be leading from the front as a servant leader. If they really want to help America in the greatest way, giving back in a decentralized and wide-spread manner is a powerful action (See the next chapter, *The Transformative Power of Giving Back*). If wealthy donors truly want to make positive changes happen quickly and leave a legacy, I would challenge them to give back via the method in the following chapter.

They also could spread the news about this new method of giving back to retired millionaires and billionaires in familiar social circles. While there are other systems for the wealthy to give back and leave a legacy out there, I believe this system is likely the best. Start a true legacy of giving back to American communities. While corporate charitable foundations should no doubt contribute back, individual wealthy citizens have even a greater opportunity to revive American communities. Both corporations and wealthy citizens have a special responsibility to give back in a way that can help sustain America. If they are truly ready to do this, I would challenge them to at least consider the system of giving mentioned in the following chapter.

Nations learn that manipulating their money supplies and interest rates for over a decade straight will result in lower demand for their treasuries. The yields have been driven so low that they do not provide safe haven from inflation anymore. When treasury yields don't provide safe haven, the only other place to go during a recession are hard assets and cash. If hard assets decline too much in value, only cash will provide a safe haven. This sets up a great depression like scenario up. We can prevent this from happening with wiser government spending and a minimum wage formulation.

Even a mighty nation can start to become short on credit relative to its ongoing liabilities. Without having invested back into its people on an ongoing basis, a nation at some point cannot sustain a strong growth rate because its people physically and technologically cannot support more growth. Americans are too heavily dependent on capital spending for production efficiency improvement. Having worked in manufacturing for seven years now, I know there is hundreds of billions of dollars on the table in efficiency improvements across America that don't even require capital investment.

We've gotten terrible at actually using mathematics to model efficiency improvement. I've worked with many engineers coming out of our finest universities. The common theme I see is that they literally are not that good at applied math. They are good at applying memorized formulas to an application that is exactly the setup they've been taught; but they are not good at new solutions that require creativity.

Our universities aren't mentoring these kids the way they need to be. Part of it may be kids are simply not working with their hands enough as young children. Physical labor combined with education teaches a kinesthetic component of learning unavailable through a few projects completed during college. Kinesthetic learning over decades creates skilled applicators of technology.

Simply put, we need our kids to work with their hands more growing up.

While the skillful application of technology is important to creating greater productivity, the simple lack of proper physical infrastructure such as roads, public transportation, bridges, and water systems can ultimately cap economic growth. What can also be said is that GDP growth in and of itself does not necessarily mean healthy physical, technological, or intellectual growth for a nation. That is evident when a nation goes into a recession. Recessions are a natural part of the business cycle and if a nation has deeper and deeper recessions, it is a sign that it does not have a strong and healthy domestic economy capable of sustaining itself through hard times.

The Question Concerning Universal Healthcare

Our nation is torn concerning the question of whether it should provide universal healthcare coverage for citizens. Lower-income as well as more politically liberal individuals seem to support the idea while wealthier and more conservative individuals oppose the idea. Like a lot of political platform issues America is struggling with today, this is a common example of just how polarized America has become. Instead of using a commonsense approach and trying to find common ground, both sides act as if the other side is trying to ruin the country. Both sides are wrong.

There are major issues that our government has allowed to occur within our healthcare industry that has made healthcare less affordable for a lot of families. Our government should own this problem. It's not just due to Obamacare. Healthcare costs were skyrocketing long before Obama took office. We know our healthcare providers will lie to us and the pharmaceuticals in conjunction with the healthcare industry have pushed pain killers onto Americans costing hundreds of thousands of American lives.

That was for one thing and one thing only, money. We know the healthcare industries are raving greedy when it comes to money and they use lobby injected regulation to protect their turfs. We have to regulate them better. It's the government's lack of high-quality regulation that we can ultimately say was a great contributor to all of those American deaths. That's a fact. Regulations are now changing to try and catch up; but, shame on American government for dropping the ball on this.

Just because America is highly regulated doesn't mean it has good regulation. Insider lobbyists wrote a lot of the regulations Congress has passed in the last 40 years. We have got to own our results. And, in the last 40 years, our regulation of the healthcare industry has been head-over-heels full of filler trash as created by the lobbyists in return for campaign funds it has given out to our federal politicians. Look up all the healthcare company donations to current campaigns of our federal legislatures. They are great in number and magnitude, more so than many other industries.

Shame on those U.S. Representatives and Senators for being in bed with these large companies that literally contributed to hundreds of thousands of American deaths. A President takes an oath-of-office to defend America against foreign and domestic threats. When companies start contributing to the deaths of hundreds of thousands of Americans for money, I think they categorize themselves as in the boat of potential threats to America itself.

With that being said, better regulation is a requirement of better healthcare. It's not the volume of regulation specifically that matters, it's the content of what's inside. Is the regulation refined enough to force proper competition and prevent regional healthcare providers from splitting up and cornering the regional markets within the U.S. acting as oligarchies for the industry by fixing prices? If it is not, you end up with pills that cost $1000 each and crap like that. What the heck! Don't we know up at the top that if we let greed take over it will? Long-term career politicians such as Nancy Pelosi, Joe Biden, and Elizabeth Warren should own this issue as a great failure on their part to influence better business within America during the last 40 years of their careers. They have been instrumental in creating the legislation we have today. Shame on them.

I am going to offer some commonsense advice. These companies are unduly influencing our government in order to corner regional markets and fix prices. In addition, we need to provide fallbacks for healthcare at the national level where states can't get away with fixing fallback healthcare program premiums for their most vulnerable citizens either. Here is my advice that aims for common ground on the healthcare issue:

1. Regulate the Healthcare industries better. This means preventing the regional healthcare providers, hospitals, health insurance companies, and pharmaceuticals from hiding oligarchies by splitting up geographical areas and forming truces to control specific regions. They do this regularly and push prices higher with this method. This also means getting into the weeds on the regulation of specific critical drugs for safety and price affordability to protect Americans. If life-savings drugs can be safely imported via the proper control of quality, stopping that importation is only hurting Americans. A few shipments that have been sabotaged purposefully shouldn't reflect on the overall process. Don't think about what the businesses in the U.S. want concerning this, think about what Americans actually need.

2. Provide a fallback national healthcare insurance plan that is based on specific criteria to be eligible. The plan would be to ensure states are not fixing the prices of their states' healthcare premium options too high in order to make money off their citizens. The criteria could simply be along the lines of: those without an employment plan option due to a loss of job, those in which the employment plan is too costly based off the specific region's norms, and those that need care such as the elderly, disabled, or mothers and children etc. (which usually are covered already under federal welfare plans).

3. Regulations (a lack of qualification for tax relief) on businesses of a certain size that do not provide affordable healthcare to their employees is going to be a required element for the federal fallback plan to work. Penalties like this help lower national costs of healthcare by creating a more competitive and level playing field among providers.

4. Regulations are needed that require all providers to detail the cost of care between businesses as well as to their customers.
5. Governors and federal legislatures: Stop letting healthcare lobbyists inject toxic policy into federal and state regulations that let them have the ability to fix pricing in their regions.

Any government must invest back into its people in order to grow a better tomorrow. There's a minimum threshold to upkeep key programs such as infrastructure, education, health and human services, and other governmental programs. When investment is minimalized and nongrowth programs prevail, the country's true economic strength begins to weaken. Just as homes appreciate, the value of strong infrastructure and education in the jobs of tomorrow appreciates as well. If an administration chooses not to invest heavily into these functions of a nation's well-being, they can pass this weakness off to future generations simply by spending a lot of money on the wrong things that get quick-turn-arounds to inflate the GDP.

Most quick-turn-around investments must be funneled to systems already built such as large corporations or current governmental departments. An administration can spend money quickly that way. It's much harder to plan out new developments spread out across the country that will bring dividends in the future that potentially another administration or generation could get credit for. That's where patriotism and honor come into play. It takes a lot of honor to promote programs meant to deliver long-term results for a nation. Promoting quick-turn-around programs is like eating a lot of junk food. If you're in the gym a lot and burning it off, it's ok for a while. It will build mass for you and provide the calories you need for an economy in hyper-drive mode. However, no matter the mass of muscle built, if only junk food is consumed, you will begin to be deficient in key nutrients. I've seen muscle-bound Marines collapse during a 20-mile hike due to a lack of key nutrients that finally catches up with them. That's how nations work as well. Things can *seem* fine for decades, but bad things can be brewing for their long-term health. That's where America is as a nation. We've invested poorly. The good news is that our government *can change*. We can learn to invest wisely in key nation-building functions on an ongoing basis.

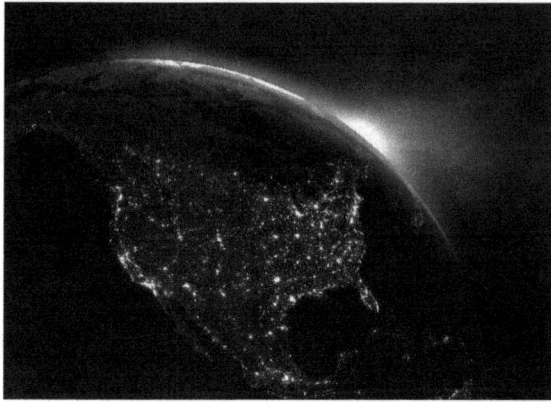

Chapter 5

The Transformative Power of Giving Back

After reading the first portion of this book, some might claim that I am prejudiced against the rich or promoting class warfare. Well, they'd be incorrect by far. In fact, I believe the potential to achieve a better way of life and accumulate wealth is a central tenant of how capitalism works. There is no incentive to work harder and smarter if one cannot benefit from it. We are a competitive species. An economic system should create an environment where that natural phenomenon is utilized to promote growth so long as fair competition can be maintained. For all its ills, America's system of capitalism is still the best thing going. It's a tough system where competition and innovation are consistently producing winners and losers. And, sometimes the winners are rewarded greatly with great wealth.

As fellow citizens, we should be happy for those who have accumulated great wealth so long as they have done it through hard work and innovation. If they have received it via generational wealth, we should be happy for them as well. It is not a crime to be wealthy or to be poor. It is our jobs as citizens to promote economics within a country that allow the poor to rise and the wealthy to fall if they manage their wealth poorly. We should promote a system that keeps economic status fluid. That is what America is all about. That is the American Dream. When one cannot better him or herself, the American Dream has become rigid and brittle.

For those who have made it to the top (families at the top 1% with incomes above $430,000 a year or a net worth above 10.4 million dollars), congratulations to you. Help your families and surrounding communities live a better life with your wealth. Be generous. Celebrate your wealth by taking care of those you love and the programs that benefit your communities. A handful of meaningful contributions per year can make all the difference in the world for schools, churches, or even neighbors next door in financial crisis due to no fault of their own. I know folks currently that are in need that work their butts off.

I remember a situation where a neighborhood father lost his wife due to her having an unexpected health issue. The family also has a daughter with a rare illness. Finding the best healthcare has become expensive for the father even though the family is well insured. Now, without a mother, the child in this family is solely dependent on the father who must work and does not have millions of dollars to invest in obtaining the best doctors in order to provide his daughter with the best chance of living a long life. It would be a God-send for a wealthy donor to walk up to their front door and drop a million dollar check off to help with taking care of the daughter. All across America, there are tens of thousands of cases like I just mentioned. All you have to do is open your eyes and start talking to the hospitals, churches, schools, and surrounding community members to find these people. Beyond this, there are millions of organizations that promote good deeds across the country. Most are worthy causes. Once you've made it to the top in America, do your best to give back to these worthy causes.

Now, for those who have made it to the very top (families at the very top 0.1% with a net worth of over 43 million dollars or individuals with a net worth of around 30 million dollars or over), congratulations to you as well. Many families and individuals with this type of net worth already give back to worthy causes for our hospitals, schools, churches, and community out-reach programs. Thanks to those who do. I would like to propose a way of giving for the top 0.1 percent of wealthy families and individuals that is likely different from what they've heard before.

It is sometimes necessary to give huge sums of money to organizations such as hospitals or foundations doing good work. Sometimes these organizations can do much good such as organizations like Saint Jude's Hospital's Make-A-Wish foundation. Other wealthy donors have donated to organizations that are attempting to find a cure for diseases such as HIV/AIDS as well as malaria. These folks truly are making the world a better place. However, I would like to say as a statistician, on average, giving massive amounts of money to a single or a few organizations is not the way to go. This is because as a statistician, I believe in the power of random and dispersed growth.

It is not easy to explain the idea of random and dispersed growth. The way I can explain it is that when a planter goes to seed a field with seeds such as grass seeds, he or she uses a seed disperser to create an even distribution of seeds across the field. In that way, the seeds are not competing for space to grow. This can apply to human development as well. A wealthy donor that gives to 10 organizations that are attempting to find a cure for a specific type of cancer is likely more apt to influence great change because of human nature. Some hard-driving intern or seasoned researcher pulling an all-nighter in a little-known research lab likely could find a cure for a major disease. These types of people are spread out everywhere. There is no rhyme or reason to how you find them.

Top-tier labs have these types of people as well as the small labs in isolated parts of the country. This is the first reason why a wealthy donor distributing support to a wider variety of programs and people on average can do more good than a wealthy donor that gives massive amounts of money to one or two organizations. A second reason why massive amounts of money given in just a few places is likely to produce slower growth is because of the phenomenon of production blocking. This is a phenomenon I am well familiar with due to working in manufacturing for the last seven years.

Large amounts of money must be handled carefully, and most large organizations put it into an account or trust that has strict internal policies on how it can be distributed. This creates a second tier of processing or what we call in manufacturing, a bottleneck. While this oversight helps ensure less misappropriations and fraud, there is no guarantee with a small or large organization that misappropriation or fraud will not occur. I would say to wealthy donors that they should do their best with promoting donations to good organizations both large and small. They should not worry so much about fraud and misappropriations.

Part of giving is taking risks just like the hard risks they took when building their businesses. With no great risks, there are no great rewards. It's really all about the time value of the seeds you plant. See, this isn't about protecting the money. It's about getting as much help as soon as possible to build a collation that produces ongoing human development for good. That goodwill multiplies much faster with multiple engines in action producing good than one foundation or trust. With that being said, the idea of giving in a dispersed manner seems scary to a lot of donors. I understand this natural fear of making sure the money is spent correctly. I would say that much more good comes from giving in a dispersed manner than bad. Taking risks is part of truly doing good.

I have created a giving system to the best of my ability for wealthy donors. I think it reflects American society's need for charity. I believe that giving in this manner will bring huge growth in our communities and happiness to worthy individuals. It will also build a true legacy of giving back for those who give in this way. I have named the system of giving, "American LORRD Awards System" based off the fact that "LORDD" stands for "*Leader of Recovery, Research and Development.*" To qualify as a specific type of giver, the system requires certain levels of donations as well as the donations to be dispersed across a wide variety of programs within an 18-month period. Once a donor has met the criteria, he or she self-certifies that the donations have taken place by signing the applicable certificate.

It is my belief that someone who gives massive amounts of money can sign off on his or her own honor that the donations have occurred. *There is no other higher-ranking person in one's life than one's own self.* The spirit of the system is to give to a wide variety of programs and people across America that are most in need. It will take some planning to give in this way. For giving at the higher levels of the system, it will take a team to distribute this amount of money properly. It's challenging. It's not as easy as giving to a handful of organizations or people.

Giving a large portion of one's net worth requires the giver to sell some of his or her assets and consolidate them into cash. This is a bitter pill to swallow for most folks that have money as it truly means that their net worth will decline after giving so much away. That's true giving. Yes, it's awesome that high net worth folks sometimes give in the millions each year so long as it does not make their net worth decline. However, it is less frequent that wealthy individuals give a large portion of their fortunes away nearly all at once. It's challenging but it can be done. Many wealthy individuals wait until later in life to give much of their wealth away. I would encourage younger millionaires and billionaires to consider giving more away in order to be able to see the fruits of their labor at work for decades before the ends of their lives.

At the end of the day, anyone that gives a large amount of money across America in this manner and actually gets hands on with the organizations and people receiving the gifts will be greatly rewarded. They will be rewarded because they will see the powerful positive effects of donating to worthy causes across a large spectrum that represents society itself. I wish the folks who decide to give in this way great success and happiness with the growth they will see. I published this system under a Google Drive account with this share link:

https://drive.google.com/file/d/1y4nTeOaCij0S_IfW5cA73kbj4RIVydoQ/view?usp=sharing

The link will take you to an attachment with higher resolutions of the awards suitable for the creation of an award display. This small pamphlet only houses the awards and is available free to those individuals or companies who want to take on the challenge of giving in this way. It is a self-managed giving system. From this e-file, an included award could be printed on photo grade paper and encased in one inch of glass with a stand so all can see a memorial of the good work that has been done.

There are five levels of giving that will fit the net worth of any wealthy donor. My recommendation would be for a donor to attempt the challenge of giving at one-third of his or her net worth. For example, if the donor is worth 30 to 50 million, give at the Bronze level which is 10 million. Gifts should all occur within an 18-month period in order to promote rapid growth. Those donations could be spread over three years' of taxes if begun at the end of one year. Yes, it's a lot and it is quick; but, truly building a legacy of giving back takes work. This system will allow a corporate charity foundation or a wealthy individual truly wanting to help society to build a legacy of giving back do just that. Do the most good their money could possibly do. Best wishes to those who have the courage to attempt to become a recipient of an American LORRD award:

AMERICAN LORRD

LEADER OF RECOVERY, RESEARCH & DEVELOPMENT AWARD

Bronze

For 1 Program in Each Category Below, I Gave $1 Million

For a Total of $10 Million (10 Programs)

Education
- € Scholarships
- € Schools
- € Colleges
- € Tech Colleges
- € Day Care
- € Early Childhood
- € Special Needs
- € Trade Schools/Jobs
- € Teacher Support

Human Service
- € After-School Prgm
- € Hunger Prevention
- € Victim Advocacy
- € Anti-Addiction
- € Halfway Houses
- € Homeless Shelters
- € Prison Rehab Prgm
- € LGTBQ Support
- € Suicide Prevention

Health
- € Mental Health
- € Find a Cure Prgms
- € Disease Research
- € Disease Prevention
- € Hospital Revitalize
- € Nursing Home Rev
- € Patient-in-Need
- € Anti-Drug Prgms
- € Elderly Assistance

Good Citizen
- € Anti-Bullying
- € Debate Program
- € Civics Clubs
- € City Development
- € Voter Registration
- € Police Relations
- € Disaster Relief
- € Public Broadcasts
- € Documentaries

Space Program
- € Exploration
- € Colony Research
- € College Programs
- € Space Camps
- € NASA
- € Private Foundation
- € NEO program
- € Exoplanets
- € Sun Research

Spiritual Leader
- € Anti-Violence Edu
- € Inter-Faith Prgms
- € Community Out/R
- € Support a Church
- € Missionary Support
- € Youth Groups
- € Religious Bands
- € Divinity Schools
- € Leader Scholarship

The Arts
- € Art Programs
- € Liberal Arts
- € Performing Arts
- € Galleries
- € Community Center
- € Orchestras
- € Bands
- € Music Programs
- € Art Scholarships

Environment
- € Earth Day/Trees
- € Clean Up Programs
- € Sustainability
- € Conservation
- € Agriculture Sustain
- € Wildlife Preserve
- € Animal Adoption
- € CO2 Reduction
- € Research

STEM Programs
- € STEM Scholarships
- € Schools
- € Colleges
- € Tech Colleges
- € Day Care
- € Early Childhood
- € Special Needs
- € Trade Schools

Infrastructure
- € Roads
- € Bridges
- € Dams
- € Water Systems
- € Airports
- € Trains
- € Subways
- € Electrical Grid
- € Bus/Transport

Within the last 18 months, I have given $10 Million to programs or people spread across the categories above. To the best of my ability, I have given gifts only to programs or people that have not received an AMERICAN LORRD Gift within the last 10 years. I understand this is not a legal certification below but instead, a personal one. I will certify myself on my honor that I have given to the above programs because I want to give back to communities across America to help support a better tomorrow for all. I give the above because I want to contribute in a way that can spread good work to as many deserving programs and people across my country. Sincerely,

Sign name: _____   Date: _____

Print name: _____

AMERICAN LORRD

LEADER OF RECOVERY, RESEARCH & DEVELOPMENT AWARD

Silver

For 5 Programs in Each Category Below, I Gave $2 Million

For a Total of $100 Million (50 Programs)

Education
- € Scholarships
- € Schools
- € Colleges
- € Tech Colleges
- € Day Care
- € Early Childhood
- € Special Needs
- € Trade Schools/Jobs
- € Teacher Support

Human Service
- € After-School Prgm
- € Hunger Prevention
- € Victim Advocacy
- € Anti-Addiction
- € Halfway Houses
- € Homeless Shelters
- € Prison Rehab Prgm
- € LGTBQ Support
- € Suicide Prevention

Health
- € Mental Health
- € Find a Cure Prgms
- € Disease Research
- € Disease Prevention
- € Hospital Revitalize
- € Nursing Home Rev
- € Patient-in-Need
- € Anti-Drug Prgms
- € Elderly Assistance

Good Citizen
- € Anti-Bullying
- € Debate Program
- € Civics Clubs
- € City Development
- € Voter Registration
- € Police Relations
- € Disaster Relief
- € Public Broadcasts
- € Documentaries

Space Program
- € Exploration
- € Colony Research
- € College Programs
- € Space Camps
- € NASA
- € Private Foundation
- € NEO program
- € Exoplanets
- € Sun Research

Spiritual Leader
- € Anti-Violence Edu
- € Inter-Faith Prgms
- € Community Out/R
- € Support a Church
- € Missionary Support
- € Youth Groups
- € Religious Bands
- € Divinity Schools
- € Leader Scholarship

The Arts
- € Art Programs
- € Liberal Arts
- € Performing Arts
- € Galleries
- € Community Center
- € Orchestras
- € Bands
- € Music Programs
- € Art Scholarships

Environment
- € Earth Day/Trees
- € Clean Up Programs
- € Sustainability
- € Conservation
- € Agriculture Sustain
- € Wildlife Preserve
- € Animal Adoption
- € CO2 Reduction
- € Research

STEM Programs
- € STEM Scholarships
- € Schools
- € Colleges
- € Tech Colleges
- € Day Care
- € Early Childhood
- € Special Needs
- € Trade Schools

Infrastructure
- € Roads
- € Bridges
- € Dams
- € Water Systems
- € Airports
- € Trains
- € Subways
- € Electrical Grid
- € Bus/Transport

Within the last 18 months, I have given $100 Million to programs or people spread across the categories above. To the best of my ability, I have given gifts only to programs or people that have not received an AMERICAN LORRD Gift within the last 10 years. I understand this is not a legal certification below but instead, a personal one. I will certify myself on my honor that I have given to the above programs because I want to give back to communities across America to help support a better tomorrow for all. I give the above because I want to contribute in a way that can spread good work to as many deserving programs and people across my country. Sincerely,

Sign name: _____ Date: _____

Print name: _____

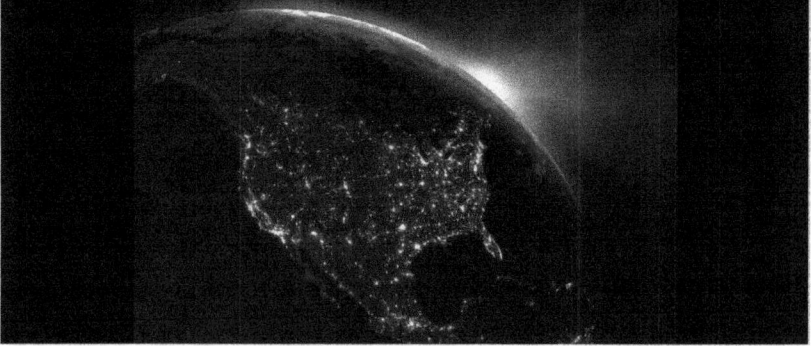

AMERICAN LORRD
LEADER OF RECOVERY, RESEARCH & DEVELOPMENT AWARD

Gold

For 20 Programs in Each Category Below, I Gave $5 Million

For a Total of $1 Billion (200 Programs)

Education
- € Scholarships
- € Schools
- € Colleges
- € Tech Colleges
- € Day Care
- € Early Childhood
- € Special Needs
- € Trade Schools/Jobs
- € Teacher Support

Human Service
- € After-School Prgm
- € Hunger Prevention
- € Victim Advocacy
- € Anti-Addiction
- € Halfway Houses
- € Homeless Shelters
- € Prison Rehab Prgm
- € LGTBQ Support
- € Suicide Prevention

Health
- € Mental Health
- € Find a Cure Prgms
- € Disease Research
- € Disease Prevention
- € Hospital Revitalize
- € Nursing Home Rev
- € Patient-in-Need
- € Anti-Drug Prgms
- € Elderly Assistance

Good Citizen
- € Anti-Bullying
- € Debate Program
- € Civics Clubs
- € City Development
- € Voter Registration
- € Police Relations
- € Disaster Relief
- € Public Broadcasts
- € Documentaries

Spiritual Leader
- € Anti-Violence Edu
- € Inter-Faith Prgms
- € Community Out/R
- € Support a Church
- € Missionary Support
- € Youth Groups
- € Religious Bands
- € Divinity Schools
- € Leader Scholarship

Space Program
- € Exploration
- € Colony Research
- € College Programs
- € Space Camps
- € NASA
- € Private Foundation
- € NEO program
- € Exoplanets
- € Sun Research

The Arts
- € Art Programs
- € Liberal Arts
- € Performing Arts
- € Galleries
- € Community Center
- € Orchestras
- € Bands
- € Music Programs
- € Art Scholarships

Environment
- € Earth Day/Trees
- € Clean Up Programs
- € Sustainability
- € Conservation
- € Agriculture Sustain
- € Wildlife Preserve
- € Animal Adoption
- € CO2 Reduction
- € Research

STEM Programs
- € STEM Scholarships
- € Schools
- € Colleges
- € Tech Colleges
- € Day Care
- € Early Childhood
- € Special Needs
- € Trade Schools

Infrastructure
- € Roads
- € Bridges
- € Dams
- € Water Systems
- € Airports
- € Trains
- € Subways
- € Electrical Grid
- € Bus/Transport

Within the last 18 months, I have given $1 Billion to programs or people spread across the categories above. To the best of my ability, I have given gifts only to programs or people that have not received an AMERICAN LORRD Gift within the last 10 years. I understand this is not a legal certification below but instead, a personal one. I will certify myself on my honor that I have given to the above programs because I want to give back to communities across America to help support a better tomorrow for all. I give the above because I want to contribute in a way that can spread good work to as many deserving programs and people across my country. Sincerely,

Sign name: _____   Date: _____

Print name: _____

60

AMERICAN LORRD
LEADER OF RECOVERY, RESEARCH & DEVELOPMENT AWARD
Platinum

For 100 Programs in Each Category Below, I Gave $10 Million

For a Total of $10 Billion (1000 Programs)

Education
- € Scholarships
- € Schools
- € Colleges
- € Tech Colleges
- € Day Care
- € Early Childhood
- € Special Needs
- € Trade Schools/Jobs
- € Teacher Support

Human Service
- € After-School Prgm
- € Hunger Prevention
- € Victim Advocacy
- € Anti-Addiction
- € Halfway Houses
- € Homeless Shelters
- € Prison Rehab Prgm
- € LGTBQ Support
- € Suicide Prevention

Health
- € Mental Health
- € Find a Cure Prgms
- € Disease Research
- € Disease Prevention
- € Hospital Revitalize
- € Nursing Home Rev
- € Patient-in-Need
- € Anti-Drug Prgms
- € Elderly Assistance

Good Citizen
- € Anti-Bullying
- € Debate Program
- € Civics Clubs
- € City Development
- € Voter Registration
- € Police Relations
- € Disaster Relief
- € Public Broadcasts
- € Documentaries

Spiritual Leader
- € Anti-Violence Edu
- € Inter-Faith Prgms
- € Community Out/R
- € Support a Church
- € Missionary Support
- € Youth Groups
- € Religious Bands
- € Divinity Schools
- € Leader Scholarship

Space Program
- € Exploration
- € Colony Research
- € College Programs
- € Space Camps
- € NASA
- € Private Foundation
- € NEO program
- € Exoplanets
- € Sun Research

The Arts
- € Art Programs
- € Liberal Arts
- € Performing Arts
- € Galleries
- € Community Center
- € Orchestras
- € Bands
- € Music Programs
- € Art Scholarships

Environment
- € Earth Day/Trees
- € Clean Up Programs
- € Sustainability
- € Conservation
- € Agriculture Sustain
- € Wildlife Preserve
- € Animal Adoption
- € CO2 Reduction
- € Research

STEM Programs
- € STEM Scholarships
- € Schools
- € Colleges
- € Tech Colleges
- € Day Care
- € Early Childhood
- € Special Needs
- € Trade Schools

Infrastructure
- € Roads
- € Bridges
- € Dams
- € Water Systems
- € Airports
- € Trains
- € Subways
- € Electrical Grid
- € Bus/Transport

Within the last 18 months, I have given $10 Billion to programs or people spread across the categories above. To the best of my ability, I have given gifts only to programs or people that have not received an AMERICAN LORRD Gift within the last 10 years. I understand this is not a legal certification below but instead, a personal one. I will certify myself on my honor that I have given to the above programs because I want to give back to communities across America to help support a better tomorrow for all. I give the above because I want to contribute in a way that can spread good work to as many deserving programs and people across my country. Sincerely,

Sign name: _____   Date: _____

Print name: _____

AMERICAN LORRD

LEADER OF RECOVERY, RESEARCH & DEVELOPMENT AWARD

Triple-Platinum

For 300 Programs in Each Category Below, I Gave $10 Million

For a Total of $30 Billion (3000 Programs)

Education
- € Scholarships
- € Schools
- € Colleges
- € Tech Colleges
- € Day Care
- € Early Childhood
- € Special Needs
- € Trade Schools/Jobs
- € Teacher Support

Human Service
- € After-School Prgm
- € Hunger Prevention
- € Victim Advocacy
- € Anti-Addiction
- € Halfway Houses
- € Homeless Shelters
- € Prison Rehab Prgm
- € LGTBQ Support
- € Suicide Prevention

Health
- € Mental Health
- € Find a Cure Prgms
- € Disease Research
- € Disease Prevention
- € Hospital Revitalize
- € Nursing Home Rev
- € Patient-in-Need
- € Anti-Drug Prgms
- € Elderly Assistance

Good Citizen
- € Anti-Bullying
- € Debate Program
- € Civics Clubs
- € City Development
- € Voter Registration
- € Police Relations
- € Disaster Relief
- € Public Broadcasts
- € Documentaries

Space Program
- € Exploration
- € Colony Research
- € College Programs
- € Space Camps
- € NASA
- € Private Foundation
- € NEO program
- € Exoplanets
- € Sun Research

Spiritual Leader
- € Anti-Violence Edu
- € Inter-Faith Prgms
- € Community Out/R
- € Support a Church
- € Missionary Support
- € Youth Groups
- € Religious Bands
- € Divinity Schools
- € Leader Scholarship

The Arts
- € Art Programs
- € Liberal Arts
- € Performing Arts
- € Galleries
- € Community Center
- € Orchestras
- € Bands
- € Music Programs
- € Art Scholarships

Environment
- € Earth Day/Trees
- € Clean Up Programs
- € Sustainability
- € Conservation
- € Agriculture Sustain
- € Wildlife Preserve
- € Animal Adoption
- € CO2 Reduction
- € Research

STEM Programs
- € STEM Scholarships
- € Schools
- € Colleges
- € Tech Colleges
- € Day Care
- € Early Childhood
- € Special Needs
- € Trade Schools

Infrastructure
- € Roads
- € Bridges
- € Dams
- € Water Systems
- € Airports
- € Trains
- € Subways
- € Electrical Grid
- € Bus/Transport

Within the last 18 months, I have given $30 Billion to programs or people spread across the categories above. To the best of my ability, I have given gifts only to programs or people that have not received an AMERICAN LORRD Gift within the last 10 years. I understand this is not a legal certification below but instead, a personal one. I will certify myself on my honor that I have given to the above programs because I want to give back to communities across America to help support a better tomorrow for all. I give the above because I want to contribute in a way that can spread good work to as many deserving programs and people across my country. Sincerely,

Sign name: _____   Date: _____

Print name: _____

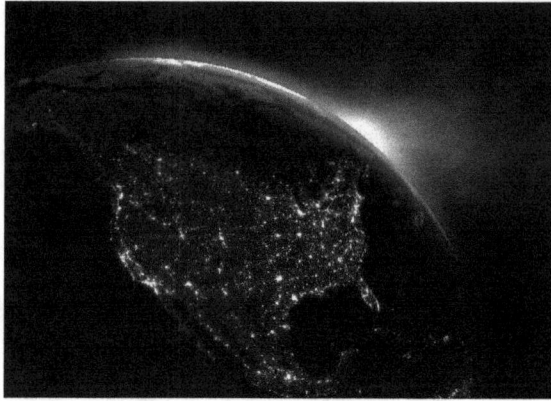

Chapter 6

SCOTUS' Failure to Protect the Republic

As it turns out, the massive monetary waste over the last 40 years primarily benefited two groups: The U.S. Government and the ultra-wealthy. While this has been blatantly apparent, nothing seemingly can be done. If large corporations can donate unlimited amounts of money across state lines, only the candidates within the smaller states that align themselves with the wealthy donors (potentially of other states) will likely be able to succeed making it through the primaries. When a handful of organizations across the United States can control which candidates make it as the accepted front runners, they pretty much control the election process. The outcome of the Supreme Court allowing large corporations to donate large sums of money to local, state, and federal elections outside of their home states is increased political conflict in our local elections. It is unfathomable that our Supreme Court Justices would support a political scheme that allows for the circumvention of the intentions of the U.S. Constitution on election management. Our electoral process is supposed to give state citizens the power of the vote and to *establish political parties at the state level, not federal level.* The Founding Fathers created state and federal offices as a way of separating powers in order to *provide for differing liberties for citizens of individual states.* Even for federal elections, the states are supposed to have the power of influence, not outside-of-state entities. Each American being bound by their individual states' laws has been handily enforced by SCOTUS for 200 years. If citizens are bound by their individual states, how can a few outsiders from other states be allowed to dump billions into local elections of states around the U.S. to influence elections? This is a flawed process. Corporations donating millions and sometimes billions to influence inter-state elections is unconstitutional. It doesn't make it constitutional just because SCOTUS establishes it as legal. This has been established in the past when future members of SCOTUS had to overturn previous rulings as unconstitutional.

Part of the reason some of the Founders wanted each state to have two senators each is that they wanted power to be spread out and not entirely decided by population alone. This would encourage development within states. And, this setup would ensure all states be given the opportunity to contribute to federal law. In opposition to this, suppose you have a corporation in which most of its workers support one political party. However, the board of directors and shareholders support another. A corporation creates wealth through the labor of its employees. Therefore, when the corporation donates massive amounts of money to a political party that is inconsistent with its actual employees' beliefs, it is creating an inequity in democracy. It is using the efficiencies created by the labor of its members, most of whom may not support a specific political party or cause, to promote the cause of just a few who hold power within the corporation. This is *violating the constitutional rights of all opposing members within the corporation to not support a specific political cause.* In fact, in most cases most employees of corporations aren't even told who the corporation is donating to prior to the donations being made. The corporation has become a de facto political entity enslaving its members to work to create wealth that supports a political party in which individual members *may not want to support.* This is a circumvention of democracy. This is why donations to political parties must be tied to individual citizens or at a minimum, the employees of a corporation should be consulted with and agree to the corporate donation! If you are using the labor of employees to create wealth, then creating political power from the distribution of that wealth to political entities not approved of by those employees, you are circumventing the very system the U.S. Republic sets up in order to ensure we have a representative form of government.

Many times, the money is used to influence out-side-of-state elections as well. This is illegal on the basis it is essentially money laundering. No one really keeps up with everything going on with this money. You hear of cases all the time of campaign money being used in all sorts of ways from Vegas trips to buying personal items. That's still not the biggest issue though with it. By forcing people to pay wealth to political parties though corporations that do not receive authorization from their employees (only through their autocratic boards who really don't have open elections) you have created an autocratic system that is not democratic. Further, this system funnels money across state lines to influence other states' local and state-level elections. *This behavior left unchecked will tear down the American Republic.* It cannot be said that the corporate board is democratic. A hand full of corporate insiders control who makes the ballot for board membership most of the time. You know this SCOTUS. Wake up. This is basically a way around the Republic-structured democracy all together.

Legal methods for corporations founded by private citizens to elect their members are not legal methods to influence elections across state lines. I would argue by this fact alone, any employee of a corporation where this is happening could successfully sue and win against this type of behavior. I also would argue that SCOTUS has the obligation to stop this behavior in the future to protect the American Republic. SCOTUS has had at least a few chances in the last 40 years to check the growing power of corporate influence in our elections process.

Instead of checking corporate behavior, SCOTUS waved their opportunity to fix this issue based off technicality. Super-PAC's and corporations that funnel money across state lines to influence elections do not pass the criteria of fair and just representative democracy. Thus, it is unconstitutional for corporations to use wealth created from all their employees (American citizens) and distribute it politically in a manner inconsistent with its total *members' will* who are not being informed of the political intent of the corporation. *This is absolutely unconstitutional* and a stain on the SCOTUS bench for allowing to happen. It is unconstitutional in all regards and the Founding Fathers would strike it down in a heartbeat. SCOTUS's reputation for generations to come rests on making this right.

The efforts of state citizens should ultimately determine who their politicians are. The Founders created it this way for a purpose. No wonder the political discourse has become so vitriolic over the last 20 years. Corporations are dumping billions of dollars into out-of-state, state and local elections tearing down the civility and collaboration of local communities. This is anti-religious as well. It is essentially creating a nationalistic system in which only political issues at the federal level matter. Local communities of a particular faith have no say and are run over in the process creating no shelter from the political strife.

The Founding Fathers explicitly provided structures to stop this from happening with the separation of local, state, and federal powers. They did this with wisdom in order to subdue conflict occurring among the wealthy and confine it to within each state as much as possible. This allows state communities to be protected in sort of a way, with the wealthy of each state vying for power rather than the wealthy collaborating and vying *for all states' power*. The spread of technology has made it ever more important for SCOTUS justices to recognize the threat that a nationalistic consolidation of power that a combination of technology and the funneling of campaign money across state lines can allow for.

This underlying structure that has rapidly been built within America in the last 40 years is taking power away from the states and can have detrimental effects on the development of our local communities as well as the federal system of our Republic itself. It naturally targets communities that are not aligned with the agenda of whatever outside donor decides to contribute across state lines to influence the congressional district election. Across-state-lines federal congressional districts are now being systematically targeted via the use of technology. The spill over of the conflict at the federal level into the heart of our local communities is toxic.

Citizens within a specific state should elect their own politicians. At a minimum, no wealthy donor should be able to donate to the political party of a state whatsoever unless he or she is a citizen of that state for a certain amount of time prior to a specific election. That rule would stop this buying state and local elections crap going on that SCOTUS has allowed to flourish. Politicians would then have to establish a dialogue with the citizens of their states to stay in office. That is how it is supposed to be. Now-a-days, politicians can just run ads from their political party's out-of-state money. Many of them hardly even have to campaign for in-state money. This is taking power away from the state citizens all together to determine their own destiny. The Founding Fathers were wise in the fact that they wanted local communities to grow somewhat buffered from the political conflict occurring at the federal level.

The Supreme Court has given the nod to an election system where most federal lawmakers are codependent on the ultra-wealthy in order to be on the ballot on election day. This system circumvents the Founding Father's intention for free and open elections and essentially creates an oligarchy with an autocratic election process. While the two political parties using the money of Super-PACs promote irreconcilable cultural differences among their followers, the results of their economics are consistently the same output for most Americans, stagnant wages for about half of Americans that support a consolidation of wealth at the top. I would hope that the SCOTUS justices do not make their decisions based off obligations they feel toward those who have helped seat them on the bench. I would hope not. I do feel there are judges with integrity on both sides of the political aisle within the SCOTUS. It's not supposed to have an aisle but unfortunately, it does. Whatever the reasoning for SCOTUS heavily protecting corporations' rights to circumvent the American election process, their decisions as of late have not made us a stronger nation. The Court will have to readdress this ongoing issue bleeding the Republic if we are to be able to believe in our current political system's autonomy to express the *will of the people*.

In the interim, I believe that state Governors have the authority to stop all flow of monies entering their states from all political entities not established in their own states. This could happen tomorrow if the Governors wanted it. No out-of-state contributions should be allowed. Then, democracy could work in a more meaningful way. Federal lawmakers will challenge Governors' authority to do this with federal election money. However, even in federal elections, the political party charters are established at the state levels. Therefore, from a legal perspective, I believe state Governors have the authority to stop all flow of campaign money, both inter-federal and inter-state, that does not originate in their home states. Yes, there would be corruption inside states as there always has been. However, the capacity for corruption is drastically limited this way (exactly what the Founding Fathers intended).

State elections would hinge on monies collected from within the state and the campaigns would then be directed toward the people of the state *with contributions given by the citizens* (wealthy or poor but still citizens of the state). We would then have a Republic made of state Republics again instead of a nationalistic system tearing our democracy apart. The massive flow of money in the last 40 years supporting inter-federal and inter-state elections has transformed our historic Republic into a bickering European-like nation-state that is tearing our Republic apart. State Governors have the authority right now to stop this! Protect our states from outside-of-state campaign influences that are unconstitutional. Freeze any and all bank accounts associated with campaign funds funneling money into your states. Fight hard at the federal court level when political and unlearned judges rule against you with the task you must do.

Appeal at the federal level pushing the fight to the U.S. Supreme Court where it has the opportunity to rule again in favor of Americans rather than corporations. America once again then can be a Republic instead of a divided nation-state. It only takes one Governor to make this happen. Utilizing executive privilege, a governor could administratively stop the flow of funds that are essentially money laundering election funds to control outcomes of elections across state lines. The campaign influence of foreign nations from abroad (which is wrong but has always been there since the founding) is dwarfed by the inter-federal and inter-state election influences of big money in America. We need to stop these unconstitutional actions that are influencing our state and local elections.

The real issue in America today is not foreign influence over America's elections. It's the influences of big money acting as a foreign agent on the behalf of a small percentage of Americans. This is the system that Nancy Pelosi and Joe Biden are fighting so hard to maintain. This system has rewarded Nancy Pelosi and Joe

Biden greatly with long and easy careers in Washington D.C. Meanwhile, the established political system bled the average American dry while funneling money to the ultra-wealthy and the Federal Government. These folks who now speak of helping the middle-class are indeed indebted to the established political system itself. President Trump made statements that hinted at this when running for election. He said he knew how corrupt the system was and that's why he could help. The establishment doesn't want actual change. The establishment doesn't like President Trump. It is afraid of aggressive moves on behalf of the American people.

Why Impeachment now over a Single Phone Call?

There are reasons for an impeachment inquiry going on now other than a phone call where President Trump asked the Ukranian President to look into the potential criminal act of a political opponent. I think the current establishment knows President Trump would be reelected. This is the only way for them to win. It may not work but in their minds it's their only shot so why not take it.

The supposed criminal act discussed during this call presumably also happened in Ukraine. Therefore, a legal scholar could point to the fact that a U.S. President is well within his rights to ask a foreign power to investigate the illegal actions of an American citizen, political opponent or not. *There is a bigger picture here.* Big money is at stake. Both Democrats and Republicans want their Reganomic cycle reset. They want another cheap massive loan to continue to take America's bills to the middle-class and poor. They want the status quo. It's not what they say, it's what they're thinking and doing that tells you the bigger picture, "President Trump, give us what we want for foreign policy abroad and for monetary policy at home or we will oust you and get a President that will!" Last I checked, it's the American people who should be deciding who the U.S. President is.

Creating an impeachment out of a single phone call between two Presidents of two nations smacks of a setup like no other, an attempt at a bloodless coup utilizing the impeachment process. If the Senate ever approves of an impeachment based off a single phone call where a President made a request about a potential criminal incident (well within his rights to do so) and then some suggestive statements that seemed to be quid pro quo in nature, we are headed for big trouble in this country. There's nothing actually illegal about what the President said. The President wasn't forcing this foreign President to do anything and likely would be giving the mentioned support either way.

If the Senate approves of something like this with such a low threshold for "Abuse of Power", we'll become a nation where the President has very little real power including power abroad to execute our foreign policy. Foreign nations will take advantage of us and will consistently strike into the heart of the U.S. Senate's foreign policy initiatives executed by the U.S. President. We'll have foreign nations leaking phone calls of our President to the lower house frequently if they disagree with our foreign policy. Is a partisan cycle of impeaching Presidents often what we want to get into? Approve of something as flimsy as this and this is what we'll have created.

There is a bigger picture here. The Senate should protect the office of the Presidency from impeachment from something of this nature on behalf of all Americans. Otherwise, we truly are damaging the power of the Presidency and that is dangerous for all Americans. If this were a legal case before a jury, the threshold for "Abuse of Power" wasn't even approached much less breached. A jury held to standards of an American court would rule in favor of the President easily. The threshold for "Abuse of Power" was not reached.

Any foreign agents, American agents, and American politicians involved in the latest setup of President Trump should be weary of treading the line of criminal behavior. President Trump likely has the legal option to utilize American counterintelligence assets if he was being spied on. We need to get to the bottom of the setup and who was involved. I would believe a U.S. President has the legal right to take drastic actions to protect phone calls between foreign powers.

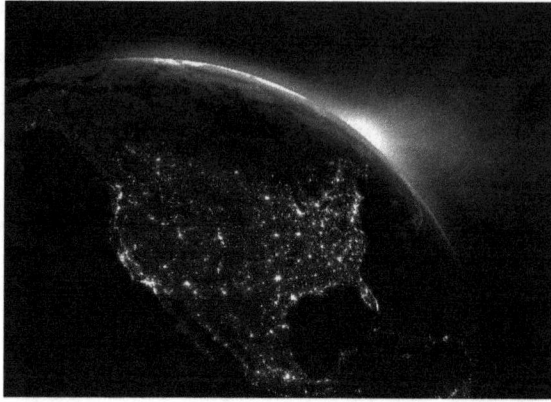

PART III

Cultural Change & Economics

"This life's hard, but it's harder if you're stupid."

-Jacki Brown
(From George V. Higgins's Novel, The Friends of Eddie Coyle)

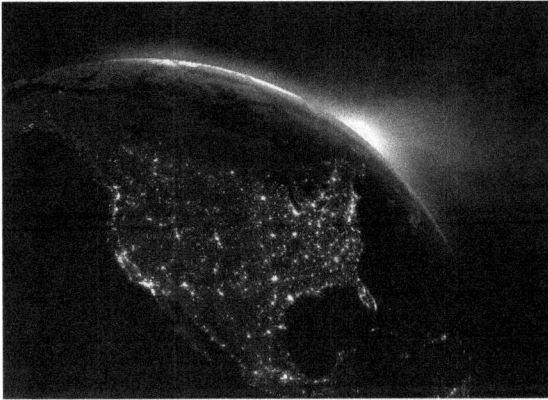

Chapter 7

Mass Shootings & Gun Control

Feeling safe in our own homes, out in town, or within our schools should be a given. Although gun violence seems to be all over the news all the time, in the last three and a half decades, gun homicides have actually declined:

Gun Homicides per 100,000 Americans 1985 to 2017

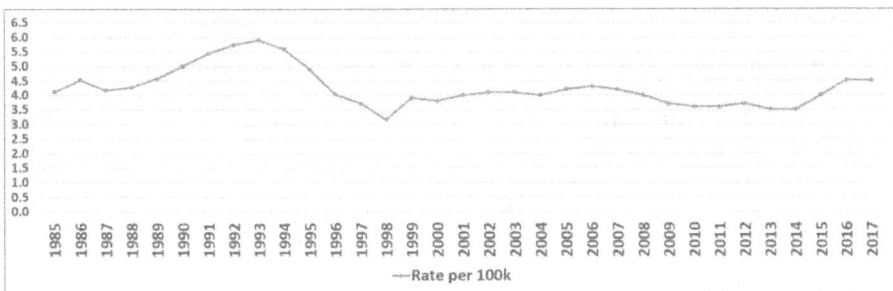

Almost all forms of violence in America—to include domestic violence, rape, child abuse, and murder—have gone down during this same time period. However, one violence trend that has increased slightly during this same period alarms citizens across the country, mass shootings. Though it is statistically improbable that a person will die in a mass shooting, the mere fact that they statistically are on the rise in America is alarming. Per the control chart below, it shows we are slightly out of statistical control for mass shootings. However, you cannot use the numbers directly without accounting for a population increase:

Mass Shooting Events per 100 Million Americans 1981 to 2018

(Analyzed with 4+ Deaths Considered Mass Shooting)

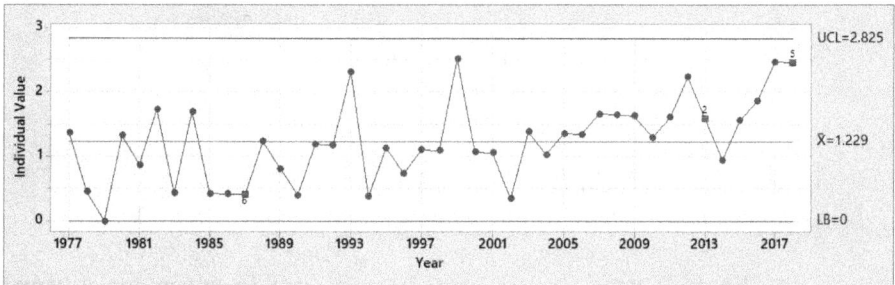

The statistical rules violated for years 2013 and 2018 are seen below:

TEST 2. 9 points in a row on same side of center line.
Test Failed at points: 37
TEST 5. 2 out of 3 points more than 2 standard deviations from center line (on one side of CL).
Test Failed at points: 42

Because it's an outlier, 1987 should be ignored. The settings of the mass shootings have also alarmed parents as more mass shooting deaths have occurred in schools. The frequency of mass shootings in our schools in the last two decades is also unacceptable (considering only shootings of four or greater):

Mass Shooting Events in American Schools 1981 to 2018

(Analyzed with 4+ Deaths Considered Mass Shooting)

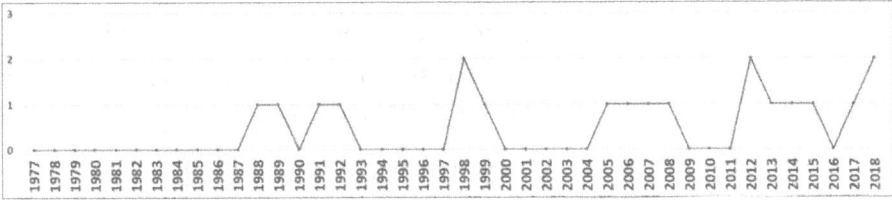

Now, as far as the severity of mass shootings concerning shootings with deaths four or greater, we also went out of statistical control as of recently starting in 2016:

Severity of Mass Shootings in America 1981 to 2018

(Analyzed with 4+ Deaths Considered Mass Shooting)

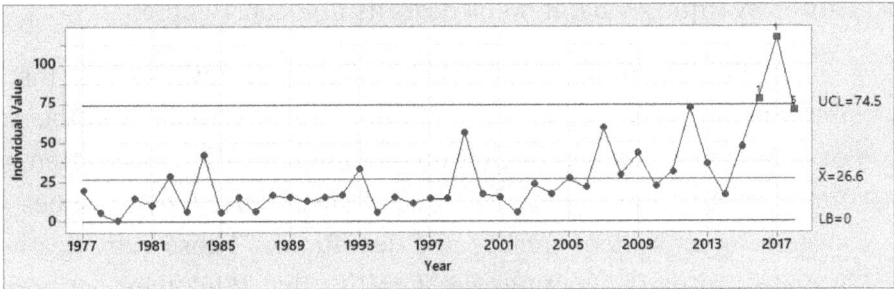

There must be contributing factors to the higher severity of the mass shootings. As a first step to reducing these occurrences of mass shootings, our government should understand the behavioral effects of our changing economics. What? Do you mean our economic makeup as a country can affect things like this? Yes. It sure can and it has. It is difficult to prove exact inputs (causal factors) to correlate to the output numbers (mass shootings) within the previous charts because the datasets are very small so any correlations would be weak at best.

We could do better as a nation though finding correlations and mitigating the few things we know that contribute to the overall increase of mass shootings. Sometimes you do not need to know the exact input variable to control the output. If there are only a handful of inputs that could be truly causing it, work on those inputs and the problem should subside and while doing so, you can better understand how the inputs effect the overall output.

In America, parents should not have to fear sending their kids to school over the occurrences of mass shootings that now occur on a regular basis in our schools. People looking to have a good time shouldn't have to fear being shot at a night club or bar either. What the heck is going on with people wanting to wreak havoc on society? What it comes down to is that someone that feels wronged or that has been wronged feels the only way to get back at society is to kill those responsible for their pain or make society suffer by killing what it holds dear, its innocent people.

From working in statistics for a while now, I know that the introduction of slightly more variation into a system from the norm over time can have significant impacts. The outlier points then get a little more extreme. It only takes a handful more of extremes in a system to get system crashes and deviations. Those extremes when it comes to mass shootings are families that *think* they are normal, but indeed, they were not due to stressors that occurred.

How about we back up and follow one of the shooters through his childhood. This kid grew up in a middle-class family. Even though this household made a good income and things *seemed* to be ok for them, this household was an extreme outlier, not even one parent was able to spend true quality time with the kids on an ongoing basis. One of their children ended up becoming a young adult that killed dozens of other children with a gun. And, the parents said to themselves, "Even good children sometimes grow up to be bad and there is nothing that we could have done about it." That may be the case for the most extreme cases involving genetic mental illness; however, *in all but a few incidents, this usually isn't the case.*

What I have noticed in these cases is that the parents were *very busy.* They may have come from different socio-economic backgrounds; but, both parents or the single parent raising the kids were very busy. Deep down, the parents look back and they know if they would have spent even an hour a day more with the kids, they could have given their kid that went bad what he needed inside to develop a sense of empathy and respect for their fellow human beings. A respect that would stay intact enough even when they were wronged or betrayed. That sense of empathy and respect for society would have checked this kid's behavior when it came to violence. It would have.

It is also not as simple as simply investigating what percentage of mass shooters had busy or preoccupied parents. What about the parents themselves? Did the parent have parents themselves that were very busy and potentially failed to pass key values, attitudes, and specific empathies along to them? For the naysayers, you don't think it's possible that cross-generational influences happen? Don't you think it's possible that certain lack of values, attitudes, or lack of empathies can be passed from a mother or father to a child unknowingly? You dang right it's possible but it's very difficult to track statistically. It's not like families that produced mass shooters sign up for a multi-generational cultural survey right after an incident.

Congressional leaders can run whatever pile of data they want to correlate factors together that have no bearing whatsoever on what affects our kids. You can find almost anything that will correlate with another factor if you search hard enough. The trick is to find the right input factors to correlate to the major output. Once you know that, you can mitigate the inputs in order to have an effect on the output. As a nation, we obviously haven't found the right inputs to control or we wouldn't be getting more mass shootings to include shootings in our colleges and schools.

If you talk to any psychologist or spiritual leader, or read any childhood development book from the last 50 years, you will find that a healthy connection to at least one parent and that parent also instilling a set of values into the kid *that included repeated reinforcement of the need to express empathy for one's fellow human beings* is what keeps a kid from going bad, period. The expression of empathy also must be demonstrated for the child by empathy being shown to him or her by the parent as well, not just the parent trying to beat it into the kid with punishment. This takes time and needs to be shown during early childhood, reinforced as the child becomes a teenager, and developed during young adulthood. Economic situations that take both parents away from their kids most of the time adds to the stressors within families.

Ultimately, all this has to do is create a few more outlier families that produce kids that become violent. It only takes a handful more of extreme outliers where certain kids did not get what they needed as far as time with an adult that was able to instill and reinforce values. Over millions of families, a few will then produce kids that migrate toward killing other kids as a form of vengeance on the society they feel doesn't accept them. They cannot empathize with society because the emphasizing mechanism within their minds is underdeveloped.

When you understand how systems behave statistically, you can apply that understanding across people systems as well. "Labor Force Participation Rates", representing leisure time parents have available to spend with their kids, is an input factor that I believe our government should pay attention to. I have found no other factor that correlates as well with mass shootings. Let's do a little bit of 8th-grade Algebra aligned with the proper inputs and outputs! Economics affect quality of life and stressors within our homes. However, you can't just correlate these two factors year to year.

Kids that grow up and shoot people take time to become mentally ill.

How about we delay the correlations 18 years and see what we get then? An 18-year delay more readily approximates the delayed fuses of our three-to-nine-year-old kids who didn't get the proper parental support at home. We used 18 years as the delay because most of the mass shootings are not due to young kids in school or even college; so, we had to create an average age for mass shooters considering older shooters as well. Therefore, we needed to shift to an average age of around 24. Issues for this child could have begun anytime during childhood or as a young adult. In statistics, you have to pick your poison when it comes to finding correlations. Therefore, we chose the most likely age severe issues for a child could have begun, age six plus or minus three years. Six plus 18 is 24 years old.

Now, I am not prejudiced concerning males or females in leadership roles in the workforce or at home. I believe a father can serve the role as primary caretaker just as effectively as a mother can. I also believe a mother can serve as head of household being the primary breadwinner, and that her husband should be able to support this in mind and spirit without delusions of a by gone era. However, historically, it has been the mothers of America doing the bulk share of nurturing children at home. Thus, if nurturing is important to the development of empathy, we must look at female workforce participation as a factor in taking time away from the nurture of kids at home. If you correlate women entering the workforce at an 18-year delay with mass shootings of three or more dead per 100 million Americans, you get pretty decent input to output trends following each other as well as input to output correlation:

U.S. Women's Workforce Participation Rates 1963-2000 Age 16+ Trended with Mass Shootings per 100 Million People 1981-2018

(Analyzed with 4+ Deaths Considered Mass Shooting)

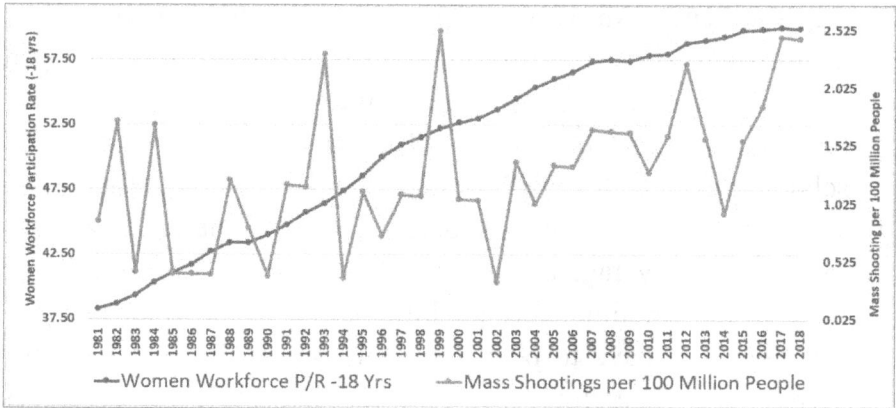

The trends above don't look like much as far as following each other perfectly. However, if you take the same chart above and you average the years in groups of three years beginning in 1981, you get a closer match:

U.S. Women's Workforce Participation Rates 1963-1998 Age 16+ Trended with Mass Shootings per 100 Million People 1981-2016

(Analyzed with 4+ Deaths Considered Mass Shooting)

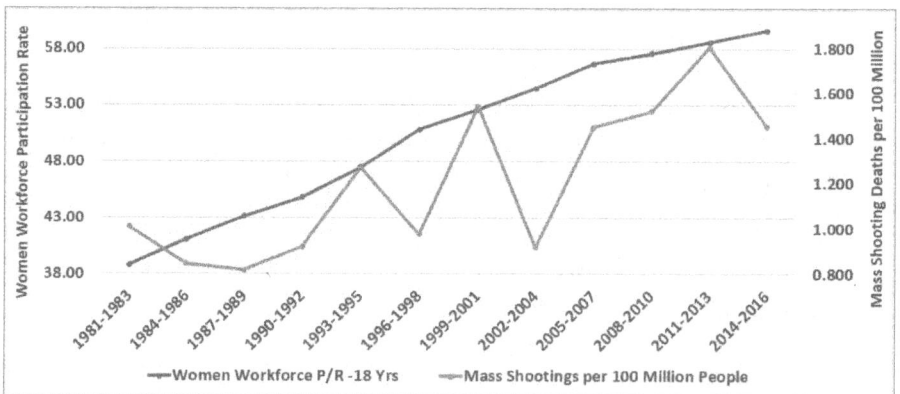

Like I stated previously, there are no perfect correlations when it comes to mass shootings. I don't have the resources to dig much deeper. But, even correlations of 25% can be important to consider if the inputs are fundamentally tied through science to worsening childhood behaviors. And, as we know, a loss of quality time with one or both parents is indeed a factor in childhood development:

Regression: U.S. Women's Workforce Participation as Predictor of Mass Shootings per 100 Million Americans 1981-2018 Age 16+

(Analyzed with 4+ Deaths Considered Mass Shooting)

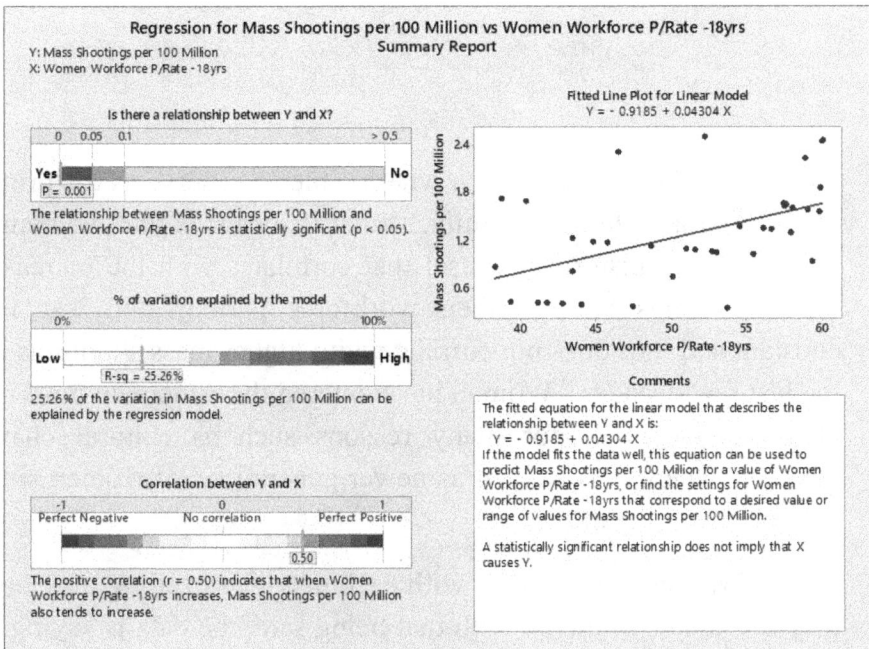

If I were to use multiple regression to see if changing male workforce participation rates also effected mass shooting rates with the same 18-year delay, no statistical significance is found. Only women's workforce participation rates correlate with significance:

<u>Multi-Regression: U.S. Men's Workforce Participation as Predictor</u>
<u>of Mass Shootings per 100 Million Americans 1981-2018 Age 16+</u>

(Analyzed with 4 Deaths+ Considered Mass Shooting)

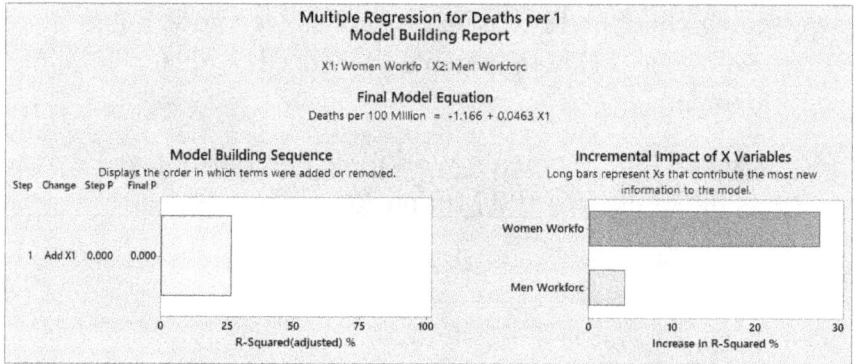

Multiple Regression for Deaths per 1
Model Building Report

X1: Women Workfo   X2: Men Workforc

Final Model Equation
Deaths per 100 Million = -1.166 + 0.0463 X1

Model Building Sequence	Incremental Impact of X Variables
Displays the order in which terms were added or removed.	Long bars represent Xs that contribute the most new information to the model.

Step Change Step P   Final P

1   Add X1 0.000   0.000

Women Workfo

Men Workforc

0   25   50   75   100
R-Squared(adjusted) %

0   10   20   30
Increase in R-Squared %

This has no bearing on whether men can serve as the primary caretake of a child successfully. What is means is that men simply do not have a historical dataset that correlates with the increase in mass shootings because their workforce participation was more constant and thus does not correlate with higher mass shootings over the last few decades. Women have entered the American workforce in greater numbers for many reasons such as cultural changes between generations as well as newer generations of women simply pursuing their dreams.

Women have proven with each new glass ceiling they break; they are equals to men. With that being said, the data is saying that mass shootings seem to be correlated with the lack of one parent being more available to the kids. I know firsthand the economic struggle facing American families and how it usually takes two paychecks now-a-days for the average American family to support their kids. Beyond this, American laws provide some of the weakest protections for parents among Western nations when it comes to allowing parents to have time off to care for kids. There are simply few federal laws that mandate parents have proper time off to support the needs and development of kids. It's a mad house sometimes with two parents working, especially with younger kids. I think we can do better as a country with this. We can provide a wider range of laws for parents to qualify for protected time off to support their kids in a variety of ways. Looking at how wealth has been being distributed in America in the last 40 years, is it any wonder why both parents are having to work so much? I can remind us of how the share of income distribution has been going with a repeat of a previous graph:

Share of Income Distribution 1980-2016

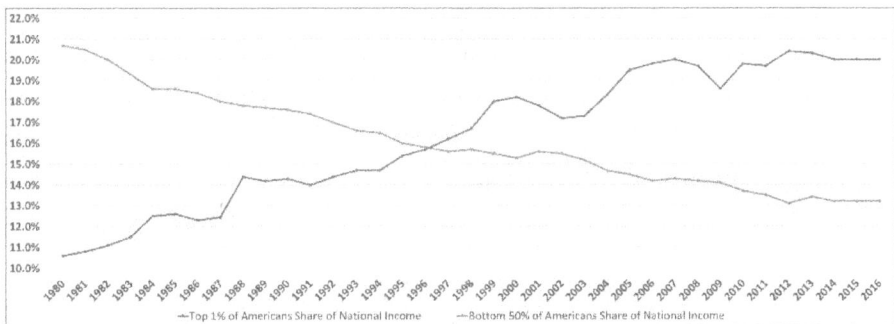

Top 1% of Americans Share of National Income   Bottom 50% of Americans Share of National Income

What this graph doesn't show is that even parents with higher incomes than the bottom 50% of American incomes are still having to work two jobs and long hours on average to pay the bills. Our nation sometimes gets carried away with tracking household income. At the same time, it fails to track other metrics that are balancing metrics against that income. For example, how many hours of combined work did both parents or that single parent put in to earn that household income? That's pretty important to show where we are going as a society.

Those combined hours dramatically increased as of the last four decades no matter the statistics the nation's bureaucracies present. Parents are also working more while at home via their cell phones and laptops as well preparing for work the next day. They are more preoccupied and not in the moment with their kids. Our nation should track total hours worked for households as a balancing metric against household incomes. This should include hours worked while at home. We could then understand the leisure time parents have to contribute to their kids' futures. *Money is not a substitute for time. Some things we don't get back.*

The good news is, if parent engagement is a key factor in mass shootings, the workforce engagement numbers of women have declined some with their peak occurring in 1999. If that is the case, mass shootings that cause four or more deaths should have begun declining in 2018 and will continue to decline slightly. Even with that being said, I don't think the workforce participation rates of women need to drop to push mass shooting numbers much lower if we can learn as a society to provide parents with the time off to truly participate in their kids' lives.

Other possible Contributors to Mass Shootings

There are a handful of other possible influencers to higher mass shootings. I'll list them. Most of them basically do one thing, make for a more chaotic home environment that may *seem normal*, but has ongoing embedded stressors on kids. Like I said before though, because we have such a small dataset with mass shootings, getting strong correlations out of any one factor isn't possible. What studies have found is that gunmen of mass shootings have a large stressor or multiple stressors occurring in their lives. Combined with this, they are greatly emotionally flawed because they cannot just cope with feelings of anger, shame, or failure that occurs in their lives in a nondestructive manner. They see their lives as essentially ruined in some facet due to circumstances potentially out of their control. So, they want to share this desperate state of mind with society. Unfortunately, they share it in a way to get the most attention they can while creating an end for themselves. It's a sad-sad loop but it's the loop we have to break as a society long before our kids become adults. We must teach our kids that just because they know they're right, or feel someone else is wrong, doesn't mean they can force their decision on society. They cannot be the judge. We have to work through society for justice. That's hard to learn especially for adolescents or young adults who believe the system doesn't care. While that sometimes is true, *life is not fair* is something they've got to accept early on:

1. *The Top Factor is a Lack of Quality Time Spent with Kids* as shown with the previous correlation of women entering the workforce. There is no doubt about this. Quality time can mean either parent but there is no substitute for time. Time ultimately means proper mentorship from an adult that is present in mind.

2. Childhood higher use of Prescription Drugs: May or may not be a key factor but is a potential influencer on how a normal brain works and can change neural pathways permanently if used heavily.

3. Higher Divorce Rates: Divorce has been shown to be extremely stressful for children.

4. Lack of Spiritual Foundation: Some type of Spiritual or ethical code that teaches it is wrong to seek revenge is huge is a child's life. There are some things you just don't do. That's what makes us human. Teach these things to your kids early on.

5. Video Games or Television/Computer Screen Time: While there have not been studies correlating screen time to the small dataset of mass shootings available, I would say that hours upon hours of screen time every day combined with other factors such as childhood use of prescription drugs and a broken or stressful home could be a factor. I think extreme violence witnessed on T.V. is also a factor depending on the age of the child as well as disposition of a child. Violence seen, real or imaginary, can affect children differently. Limiting screen time to a couple hours per school day and maybe not so much on Friday nights and Saturdays is likely a good approach to help a child's brain develop with excess induced fear or stimulation. A child needs to find other things such as music, art, outside activities, or reading/writing instead of the constant high frequency stimulation from video games or action flicks that don't require them to interact with their own decision-making faculties.

6. Modern Stress of School & College Academic Performance combined with Extracurricular Activities: Kids that don't have time to get involved

in low stress activities they enjoy other than mandated activities really never have a routine decompression period for their minds to relax. This is key to a healthy brain to learn to be creative as well as to be able to think differently in order to be able to cope during stressful situations. I was appalled to learn many schools have taken recess away from younger kids because they "don't have time" or to prevent drama from occurring between kids. This is the time kids should be learning to deal with drama and interact appropriately! Teachers should be good coaches during this time allotted to make sure kids know how to have disagreements cordially and to be able to let stuff go.

7. Modern technology: Kids needing to keep a rep up at school based off the latest one liner social network accusation or a group conversation gone wrong start to get addicted to how they feel society views them. This can be detrimental to a child's development and self-esteem. A kid that constantly is worrying about this stuff takes longer to mature and can learn to get offended easily. We have to teach our kids no matter how much money someone's parents have or not, it truly is your attitude and the content of your mind that matters. I've seen a poor kid with the heart of a noble and a rich kid with the heart of a villain. I've seen it the other way around too. Being poor or suffering doesn't make you good. The same thing goes for being rich. No kid should have the heart of a villain. Parents should teach them otherwise. *A kid with proper self-control and empathy for their fellow human beings does not grow up to become a mass shooter.* To teach these things, sometimes parents have to let go of their egos and realize that all kids need to discipline their minds. All kids are capable of participating in selfish acts, just as adults are. Stop making excuses for a child's selfishness. Teach your kids to control their emotions otherwise you're setting them up for failure due to rapidly occurring social network conversations that now occur with technology. A kid can accidently say the wrong thing now-a-days and be branded socially because of how kids repost the words of others. Teach them to be careful with their written words. And, at the same time, when group conversations do get out of hand, teach them the maturity to just be able to drop it. They can learn to ignore rumors and control tactics of other kids using shaming or group membership as leverage.

Gun Control & Attitudes Needed to Pass Meaningful Legislation

While I didn't list gun control as a factor in why mass shootings are going up, I do think America isn't the country it used to be 50 years ago. Even one deranged man getting a hold of an assault rifle with tons of high capacity magazines is just stupid on the part of the American government if we don't attempt to lower the chances of it happening. Even one mass shooting we could have prevented with sensible laws would be worth it. As a student of policy and government, I also believe based off the U.S. Constitution, an American President has the absolute responsibility and right to protect America from all enemies foreign and domestic.

If citizens killing other citizens with specific types of weapons becomes an issue, I am pretty darn sure an American President has the absolute right to protect the majority from the small minority threat of lone wolf domestic terrorism by restricting common weapons used in these types of attacks (mass shootings are indeed domestic terrorism). It is a fact that these large-scale attacks are happening slightly more often now against innocent bystanders. Therefore, a President no doubt has the executive right to control weapons used in civil unrest. That's a given despite the constitutional arguments against it trying to use the 2nd Amendment as an overarching authority. An amendment cannot nullify the overarching authority of an executive to protect an entire nation. The 2nd Amendment as superior to executive authority to protect citizens is a legal argument that will likely not hold up in the Supreme Court. *There is a bigger picture of constitutionality.* A President making a call like this doesn't stop someone from owning a gun or another hundred guns for that matter.

I was in the Marine Corps for several years and was trained in the use of assault rifles. I get the whole deal about rifles don't kill people, people do. I also know that a couple of handguns can be just as deadly as an assault rifle at close range. I grew up hunting with a shotgun and rifle by the time I was 10. However, I know the difference between a weapon system designed to kill hundreds of people and one that is not. High capacity magazines are designed to kill hundreds of people regardless of whether they feed a pistol, rifle, or shotgun.

We've recently restricted bump stocks which was a sensible step. Things sometimes have to change to make nations a safer place to live and work. Outlawing high capacity magazines (more than 20 rounds) and requiring background checks for all new gun purchases are likely good approaches to responsible gun laws. There are around 330 million people in this country now. Seventy years ago, there were only 150 million people.

We've more than doubled in less than a lifetime and things are getting crowded in a lot of places. Large groups of people are vulnerable to lone wolf attacks. That is why sometimes society does need to change as it grows. Beyond an outlaw of high capacity magazines, I see no reason why an American citizen would have a problem getting a background check done prior to buying a gun. Gun shows and private citizens who sell to anyone should pretty much be required to have seen the background check and do a bill of sale to document the transaction. With technology, validating a background check and creating a bill of sale could be made easy.

The Justifiable Fear that the NRA and Certain Gunowners Have

First off, I would like to say that I think trying to confiscate the current assault rifles that are out there is a bad move. In any operation where there may be bleeding, stopping the bleeding is the best approach. Outlawing all future sales and production of high capacity magazines and requiring background checks for all future gun purchases or exchanges is an 80% solution. Combined with this, strong regulations on holding folks responsible for securing their own guns will supplement this approach well. Trying to confiscate guns that Americans already own is the antithesis of a wise approach. Simply put, it's stupid and borders on political idiocy if you truly know how American government works. Fix the current system you have now.

Americans can secure their own weapons. Eliminate the probability that a deranged gunman can buy a gun without a red flag. How is it that some governmental officials such as Beto O'Rourke are really so picket-fence-fried that they think the average rifle owner is going to give up their gun purchased legally? It's just not going to happen. They'll help vote guys like him out of office before that happens. This approach will create a backlash from gun-owning voters ruining the chances for meaningful legislation that actually will help keep us safe.

Folks like this former U.S. Representative must have not rolled up their sleeves during their lives and worked among hard-working Americans in a way where they actually know what good Americans are made of. Hard-working Americans are better and more trustworthy people than folks like Beto O'Rourke seem to understand. They are heroes and law-abiding citizens. Literally stripping guns from their hands against their will is simply not an intelligent approach. We simply have to expect a higher level of political acumen of our federal politicians than this.

Someone that speaks well behind a microphone does not necessarily mean the person is emotionally intelligent, tenacious, and learned in American cultures, histories, laws, and economics. That is what a good American President is made of, think Abraham Lincoln or Teddy Roosevelt. American Presidents are fighters that have immense personal strength to fall back on when tough decisions have to be made and wise compromise must be made, even when personal wishes have to be put aside. *Legislative success isn't about what some (or even half) of Americans want. It's about getting legislation passed which most Americans can accept as descent policy even if it is a compromise.* How is it that I would have to remind a U.S. Representative of the greatest nation on earth that? What's wrong with our leadership today?

If we want to understand masterful legislative compromise, study how Bill Clinton worked concerning getting legislation passed. While I am not the biggest fan of President Bill Clinton, I can say factually that President Clinton had an innate ability as a human being to understand how to come together with members of the opposing political party and seek compromise to get legislation passed. Study his long sessions with Republicans and his staff working through issues to get to compromises. He would stay up all night many of a time figuring out the roadblocks to successful legislative bills. He did some decent work concerning American economics as well.

President Clinton definitely wasn't perfect; he continued Reaganomic policies and this set us up for President G.W. Bush's mismanagement of Reaganomics. However, he still sets the bar in the last few decades when it comes to collaboration between political parties. If you don't agree or believe President Clinton was the Devil, do some homework then come back to your withheld judgement. Just because we don't agree with a President's morals doesn't mean his leadership wasn't good. Relative to President Clinton, President G.W. Bush's outward morals were squeaky clean. Outward morals, or what the Bible calls "weaknesses of the flesh", do not necessarily determine what that person's inner morals are concerning being able to empathize with one's fellow human beings.

Back to the gun control issue. Look, I get it. There are situations that have occurred and unfortunately continue to occur that make gunowners wary of following more codified rules. Federal agents have been known to show up at someone's house and knock down the door to the wrong house with guns-a-blazing. Police officers have shot up vehicles of law-abiding citizens with them in the vehicle simply because the vehicle looked like a vehicle of the bad guy. Cops have shown up at an address of a supposed bad guy and killed an innocent unarmed victim on the street that they thought was him. What the heck is that? Unfortunately, it happens. Many of our police departments lack proper cultural and interaction training.

In the last few years, two ladies were awarded 4.2 million dollars because the vehicle which they were in was shot 103 times because cops thought a bad guy was in their truck. The women were out delivering newspapers and the sound of the paper hitting concrete sounded like gunfire to police. The women barely escaped with their lives. One of them was shot twice. If these women would have been cornered and the cops would not allow them to surrender, they would have had no alternative but to start firing back at the cops, hoping they were better shots in order to save their own lives. If carrying their guns legally, they would have been well within their constitutional rights to do so. Police officers are representatives of the people and when they make grave errors by attacking law-abiding citizens and literally seek to take their lives from them, those citizens have the God-given and constitutional right of self-defense.

All that being said, it is also a fact that dozens of police officers are killed in the line of duty each year in the United States. Therefore, it is highly understandable that they are quick-on-the-trigger to potential threats. I understand what it is like in a war zone where the only feeling of safety you have is your personal weapon. The cases mentioned concerning police shooting unarmed bystanders are extremely rare. However, they are representative of the real-life fears some American citizens have and to be a just contemplator, I must consider both sides. I understand the arguments from the 2nd Amendment supporters side of the camp. For them, they feel they have the constitutional right to own guns to protect themselves from all foes that are operating outside of the law. And, they believe that the American 2nd Amendment is the only document they ever should need to do that.

In either case, *I believe there is a bigger picture* when it comes to how guns should be allowed to be sold in the future in

America. Maybe we grandfather clause certain ownerships in. The President of the United States ultimately has the right to protect his or her fellow citizens and it is likely well within Presidential rights to issue executive orders to tweak gun laws. If shootings ever got too bad, a President likely has whatever authority necessary to ensure the safety of Americans and there is no doubt this authority would be backed by the U.S. Supreme Court.

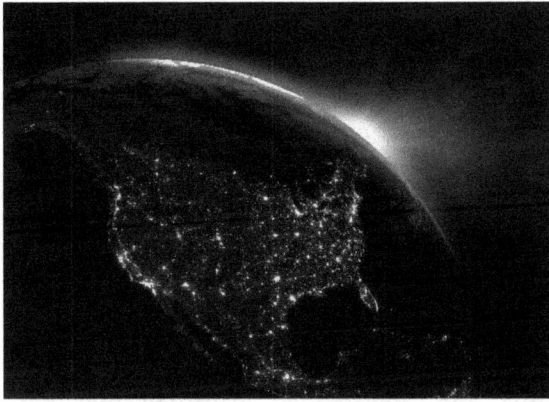

Chapter 8

National Security Policy

Evolving our National Security Policy is a cultural challenge for America because what we've done in the past isn't working anymore; yet, our cultural mentalities of the past are still well embedded. Since World War II, the Western nations have essentially been aligned militarily and economically. As global economics have changed, American leadership simply hasn't changed as quickly. The result is consistent suboptimum national security policy.

Within this chapter, I will only hit on our current hot-topic national security challenges. While I am by no means qualified to discuss most national security issues of given regions around the world, there are some areas, particularly the issues at the forefront of national security right now, that I have studied and seen the results of firsthand while in the trenches. I have also had ongoing dialogue and research going on with these issues due to my curiosities over the last 20 years, potentially much more actual empirical thought and consideration than many of our top policy makers. I also like to think it doesn't take a General, Representative, Senator, or a wealthy person to think wisely. Dwight D. Eisenhower, just five years before becoming the Supreme Allied Commander over the whole European theatre during World War II, was just a lowly Lieutenant Colonel. He only rose to power so quickly because someone noticed he had talent in strategy and wargames back in Washington D.C. While I am no Dwight Eisenhower, I would say I am capable enough at offering some corrections and improvements to some of our ludicrous and elementary attitudes that have sub-optimized American diplomacy and national security strategy in the last 40 years.

Israel and its Relationship with other Middle Eastern Nations

Around the world, almost every nation accepts Israel's right to exist and its right of sovereignty over its current borders. Nations that don't are just simply not going to win in this respect whatsoever. I would say to nations that think like this to calculate the odds against you and change or be at risk of being changed. It is just simply stupid for a nation to preach that Israel should not exist. Israel does exist. They have a powerful military with advanced technology the U.S. has highly subsidized in the last 60 years, and likely have had nuclear weapons for decades. They aren't going anywhere for the next 1000 years so governments that think differently are just fooling themselves and their own people. That's about it. Living in a world that isn't aligned at all with reality doesn't help one's people, it hurts them. Wake up and come to the table. Israel's people are phenomenal as well. They have a culture of helping hands and take care of their own. They have always been friendly and grateful to America for helping secure their place in the world. I've gotten to travel to Israel and can say the Israeli people are good people.

That being said, I think Israel can do more to promote peace in the Middle East. They must delineate the words of a few from surrounding nations' cultures and potential valuable contributions to regional trade and economic growth. Responding with brute force is not the way of the future. The whole of the planet is behind an ongoing recorder where the people of the planet are determining for themselves if the actions of nations are just or not. Israel should remember that many nations are watching concerning its methods of pursuing peace rather than attempting to escalate, destabilize in hopes of, or openly pursuing war. Israel's own people want peace as well. Peace through strength is not a bad policy. However, always responding with force is not the best policy in today's geopolitical climate either. The moral high ground is tremendously valuable and will be for the coming decades.

Saudi Arabia & Iran

Separating Saudi Arabian policy from Iranian policy is like trying to separate the chocolate chips from raw cookie dough. The operation doesn't work very well, and it gets very messy. These two countries both are dependent on oil exports and while Saudi Arabia has found favor with America in the last several decades, Iran has not since its revolution. While some say this revolution ushered in a dictatorship, other changes that occurred after the revolution actually benefited Iran's people. While Iran has had its fair share of internal political dissent, relative to other nations in the Middle East during the Arab Spring of the last 10 years, it is a nation that is relatively peaceful within its own borders.

The current situation in the Persian Gulf area right now is that Saudi Arabia is caught between a rock and a hard place. Saudi Arabia is a great nation with a beautiful country and remarkable people. I have seen this for myself. Unfortunately, Saudi Arabia is now in a situation where some of its neighboring countries are unhappy with the rulers who lead their governments. This is creating turmoil. This is combined with the turmoil being manipulated into chaos by Iranian-back insurgents. There are both terrorists organizations as well as political factions just wanting change that are causing multiple stressors throughout the region. Saudi Arabia's largest oil company, Aramco, is smart in the fact that it wants to go public with its shares and seek refuge in cash as soon as possible.

The more chaos that occurs, the lower the valuation of Saudi Arabian oil companies as well as other Saudi businesses. Most investors fear investing within a geographical region prone to the outbreak of war. That's the situation going on right now. The question is, will it come to war? And, if it does, how will it actually play out? What I can say is that having predicted the chaos of Iraq as a lowly Lieutenant in the U.S. Marines Corps many years ago, the whole situation concerning Saudi Arabia and Iran is much worse. I will do my best to describe the most likely outcomes if the conflict escalates to war. The American people have the right to know just how bad this situation could become. I think the Trump administration is more open to the realities of war than President G.W. Bush's administration was at the onset of War with Iraq.

Since the Iranian Revolution in 1979, all Presidents since Reagan have had sour relations with Iran, this includes President Obama as well. The latest issue of course is the fear of Iran acquiring a nuclear weapon. It always makes me scratch my head when you think about it. While America was attacking Iraq in 2003 which had no capability to acquire nuclear weapons, we took our eyes off North Korea and literally let them develop nuclear weapons. This is a fact. President G.W. Bush's administration let this happen. Again, no responsibility was taken by President G.W. Bush's administration for this big foreign policy fail. In either case, the world did not stop. North Korea has long had the capability to launch a nuclear weapon over the border and hit South Korea. So, why hasn't it done that? The answer is simple. It would mean the end of the North Korean regime altogether. The same thing goes for Iran.

It appears to me that American Presidents should seek help with preventing regimes like Iran from acquiring nuclear weapons because if they don't, the oncoming Presidential administration can simply let them have them like was the case with North Korea. Therefore, as bad as it pains me to say this, President Obama's nuclear arms prevention deal that included other countries supporting the effort against Iran was actually a good idea. The elements of it may have not been tough enough; but, it was a good idea. The only other alternative to this is massive obliteration of the country of Iran causing hundreds of thousands of Iranian deaths and a cascade of effects that will affect the global economy just as a start.

Afterwards, the cascade will continue likely costing tens of thousands of Saudi Arabian military and civilian lives, a decimated Saudi Arabian economy, a spike in terrorism in Israel, Europe, and America, as well as the potential loss of thousands of American military and civilian lives in the years to come. Is the need to attack Iran worth all of that? American government has an absolute responsibility to answer all these questions to the American Republic and the American people prior to attacking a country that can destabilize the world economic order and risk millions of lives globally.

I think of North and South Korea recently when escalations were very high. They actually came together collectively and stated to President Trump, they don't want war. This was very wise on both of the nations' parts. Both Saudi Arabia and Iran will lose in a war. Now, if you want to think at the base and shrewd Machiavellian levels about it, America in the mid-to-short term could actually make out if a war were to break out with Iran. Assuming America doesn't lose an aircraft carrier or large naval vessel costing thousands of American lives, it would now be the global leader in energy production and oil refining for years to come.

While chaos ensued over all the Middle East (disregarding the first six months afterwards that could potentially spiral into a global economic recession), America could actually make out (again only in the mid-to-short term economically). That's what scares me about how American oil companies and a handful of our politicians sworn to them actually think. They think they are analyzing at the strategic level like the Bush Administration was. Unfortunately, they are really thinking at the mid-to-short term operational level. Americans could lose much more than a ship or two with an attack on Iran. We could lose our future safety at home and abroad as well as the moral high ground causing America to be ostracized by many other peaceful countries that could simply democratically choose not to do business with us. We could lose the moral high ground forever. Why?

With war, we would create such a large terrain of chaos across the whole of the Middle East that small counter American factions would be the norm. These factions would now flourish throughout the Middle East—to include Saudi Arabia and Iran—and we would have no way to control them whatsoever. Think terrorists and extreme political groups that hate Americans are flourishing now? Take Iran proper out of the picture (which actually has some control over these groups) and see what happens. Believe it or not, Iran could be our biggest ally when it comes to deescalating and preventing future Islamic radicalism from spreading across the Middle East if a peaceful path forward could be found with them.

If America can't even stop the drug war which is now responsible for around 20,000 murders a year in Mexico (our next-door-neighbor), do you think we will be able to quell the post war anarchy associated with an area about the size of Mexico that is on the other side of the planet? Heck no. We still haven't in Iraq, and we wouldn't be able to in Iran. A world without Iran proper would be a world of uncharted territory with factions bleeding out in all directions with one goal in mind, finding someone to blame for creating an apocalyptic world in which they now have to live in with their children. That common foe would be America.

Hundreds of thousands of young men will have nothing to live for except for war. Saudi Arabia would see the effects of all of this first followed by Israel, Europe, then America. Ultimately in the following years, thousands of innocent Americans could also lose their lives due to renewed terrorist activities as well as the sacrifice of further troops we would likely have to send to prevent total anarchy across the Middle East. Is this the world we really want? Is this the world that our current administration wants to create by showing it can hold the line with a country from acquiring a nuclear weapon? I would say even in the event *Iran did acquire a nuclear weapon*; war with them isn't worth it.

North Korea acquired nuclear weapons over 10 years ago. It recently joined South Korea hand-in-hand stating it doesn't want war. There's zero chance Iran would use a nuclear weapon on Israel, Saudi Arabia, or America. They want it for one reason—to deter an attack on their own nation, just like all the other nuclear powers. This includes Israel, which currently possesses nuclear weapons in the shadows. Despite the rhetoric thrown around about destroying Israel, Iranian leadership wants nuclear weapons for one reason, deterrence from attack.

Our justification for preventing Iran from acquiring a nuclear weapon because they will use it on America, Israel, or Saudi Arabia is an absolute lie. We should at least recognize this as a starting point on whether or not to attack Iran simply on the premise of preventing the nation from acquiring a nuclear weapon. It's easy for someone of self-indulged or politically partisan mindset to state things such as "do you really want to chance them using it?" It is a fact they would never use it unless attacked by an overwhelming force seeking regime change (i.e. America attacking Iraq last time). Start from that point and move forward with your rationale.

I can guess that a general question occurring in the American military and political circles in the last 10 years is whether or not America should attack Iran before it continues to develop greater technological defensive capabilities to produce pain around the world in case it is attacked. That's the strategic scenario of sorts likely being thrown around in Washington D.C. I can tell you ladies and gentlemen, it's not a game to play with. It's dangerous to promote preemptive war as a viable method of international foreign policy. This mentality could lead to a destabilization of the world order and rapid global economic meltdown. Iran is not the Third Reich. We need to stop selling it as such. Last I checked, Iran was not invading neighboring countries left and right and killing its own people in the millions depending on their heritage or religion. Although they are fighting proxy wars, they are not the only nations around the world who participate in this behavior to include Western nations.

For those on the far-right side of things in America that favor war with Iran, I would like to caution you that you are not really helping Israel or America out thinking this way. Israel would suffer greatly in the years to come if there was a war with Iran. The terrorism would skyrocket for decades costing potentially tens of thousands of innocent Israeli lives. Israel's economy could also be severely damaged. Not cool. For the average American who truly wants to stay the path as a follower of Christ, we must first seek peace per several confirmations within New Testament Biblical doctrine. We should remind our war-promoting ministers who sometimes are know-it-alls that Christ's directives take precedence over their own personal opinions. If not, we are not on the side of Christ, we are instead embedded with personal spirits of ego and revenge.

Americans should start turning the T.V. off when they hear television evangelists begging for war in the Middle East. Something has gone afoul in these ministers' reasoning. *They are living in the Old Testament trying to enforce the law rather than the New Testament where we have Grace.* Americans need to stop donating money to these organizations which are promoting war in the Middle East. I assure you they are not true evangelical Christians if they awake each day wanting to call down hell fire and brimstone on other nations. I know a thing or two about true evangelical Christians and these ultra-wealthy T.V. characters don't fit the mold.

I cannot claim to be an evangelical Christian myself. I don't have the personal chastity of mind to be of such phenomenal faith. But, like I said, I know a thing or two about what true evangelicals are made of. First and foremost, they have fundamental moral values. However, those values include an unrelenting element of forgiveness toward one's fellow man with the belief they are not the judge, God is. They also truly believe that peacemakers will inherit the earth. In contrast to this spirit, a handful of T.V. evangelicals have been preaching going to war with Iran and other Middle Eastern nations as of late. What these guys really are, are just ultra-wealthy businessmen clothed in religion. They are also asking for our money to make themselves even richer than they are now. We would be better off giving locally to our local churches that actually help our communities out and stay away from characters that profess war is divine.

Most these characters have never seen a young American pumped full of morphine whimpering while he bleeds to death. Whether or not these characters are simply religious ideologues or in it just for the money, statesmen should have departed from their confidence long ago back in the American Revolution. It was then that we separated church from state. European citizens often went to war over religion. We wanted freedom of religion in America and freedom from war fought over religion. Let's listen to Christ, the better side of history, and to our Founding Fathers on this one. Christ would be on the side of the Founders who sought protection against emotional entry into war. They only departed as subjects of the British Crown after long and weary debate.

As Americans who consider themselves Christians, we need to be very wary of ministers who call for war. I am not a pacifist. There is a time for war. America has had to go to war on several occasions giving the blood of its young to defend freedom around the world. War that creates an environment worse than the pre-war environment is a waste beyond words. Bombing Iran into oblivion does not create a better post-war environment for America, Israel, Europe, Saudi Arabia, or surrounding nations. It creates a world of greater uncertainty, danger, and disconnected economic regions that will likely lead to global economic contraction and deep recession.

Another misnomer I'd like to clear up is the idea that you can't negotiate with Iranian leadership because they are untrustworthy radicals. That's the argument of the extreme religious right or political right in America. It's not the argument of a moderate Republican, Democratic, Independent or Christian. It's factually untrue. While Iran is no doubt involved in supporting proxy terrorist groups abroad, they are a disciplined bunch of people and mostly do exactly what they say they are going to do. I know this firsthand because if they were not, many of the American ships and aircraft that push the limits with their military almost daily would have been openly fired upon already. The Iranian military must have a standing order out not to fire upon any American or Western vessels or aircraft unless fired upon first even in the event these vessels or aircraft pierce territorial waters or the safety zone of its ships.

There is no doubt based on all the reports we hear concerning this topic that the American military pushes the limits of poking the eye of the Iranian military. American sailors and troops follow orders. It is unethical of our senior military leadership to put them in harm's way in an attempt to cause an international incident to provoke Iran. It's not the moral high ground. If it ever came to war, America having conducted operations such as this will likely severely damage the chances the American people would ever truly approve of a war with Iran. The American people will have seen we have no bearing to take offensive action based off losing the morality of our conduct in the Persian Gulf. We must be better than our rivals.

Attacking Iran would potentially create thousands of factions within Iran that would spread into Iraq, Jordan, Syria, Israel, Saudi Arabia and surrounding nations, and Europe with the common goal of bringing down the Saudi Arabian economy, hurting Israel, Europe, and America. It would be a stupid move. The question on the use of overwhelming force is whether it's truly just to use that force. *If our spirit inherently seeks war, something else dark has taken ground in the way we operate.* We should be modeling risks empirically rather than through attribute experiential knowledge so prevalent in Washington D.C. There are ways to mathematically model military risks posed by proxy as well as conventional military actions against an opponent. However, in my opinion, an attack against Iran in my opinion simply cannot be properly mathematically modeled as the ramifications can exceed a one-hundred-year timeline.

There are also political parties in Israel that vehemently support war with Iran. It is their right to do so. However, I sometimes think that these political parties are really not aware of the long-term strategic cost going to war with Iran would incur on their children and grandchildren. Back in 2010, some say President Obama may have surrounded Iran with the American military not because he was afraid of Iran but to prevent Israel from sneaking in offensive action through neighboring countries against Iran destabilizing the region. America may have felt that holding the cards by controlling pretty much all the airspace and securing the borders between Israel and Iran was its best option based off some type of intelligence it had received concerning a potential imminent Israeli attack.

I will not judge this move as wise or unwise if it actually did happen. What I will say is that it was indeed a brazen and unprecedented foreign relations action if it did happen. It also hasn't really been flaunted by the American National Security apparatus. Thus, it makes me think if it did happen President Obama wasn't asking for accolades. Instead, he may be content to let the historians judge him. What is likely now, is that Israel for the most part must report into American airspace or ground force communications if it decides to unilaterally take offensive action against Iran. An exception to this would be Israel using the freedom of the seas via submarines or naval vessels in the Persian Gulf or Indian Ocean to launch a sea-borne attack. This foreign policy setup makes sense to me based off America's current overwhelming presence in the regions between Israel and Iran.

If I were able to speak with Iran, I would caution them against using the plan of the destruction of Saudi Arabia as a tit-for-tat strategy in the event of an attack. Saudi Arabia is a sister nation. The best and most lasting assurance that other nations will never attack Iran is for Iran to make a lasting peace with Saudi Arabia. This is their best hope of maintaining their country's viability as a nation in the global community for decades to come. That's a bitter pill to swallow for Iran but if Iranian leaders love their own people, in the name of peace, they would swallow it without hesitation. Peace with Saudi Arabia and refraining from attacking the legitimacy of Israel or striking out at Israel would likely take the conversation away from war immediately. It would put the collective future of the region in the hands of two potentially great partners, Saudi Arabia and Iran.

All of that being said, this is the situation as guessed by an average American of little means—me. I am not privileged to any of the knowledge given to our top brass. I have seen the results of war firsthand such as the ruined national infrastructure of Iraq and young American Marines and Soldiers bleeding to death that did not get to come home to American mothers. I am an American who simply pays attention to our news and can read in between the lines a bit. The American people and our government should be aware of the *bigger picture* prior to even considering military action against Iran proper. We should not be as we were with Iraq, going in with one eye shut to the truth and hoping for the best outcome. Iraq was a country that had infinitely lesser capabilities to cause global distress than Iran currently has. Let's own our results. History judges governments and Presidential administrations by their results not their intentions.

A result of lasting peace is far superior in historical terms than dropping a lot of bombs on another nation. We do not live in a conventional world of warfare anymore where the nation that drops the most bombs ultimately is a benefactor of the decision to drop those bombs even if it wins. Destabilizing a war-torn region as large as the Middle East any further could indeed cost America its economic future. Any President can give an order to drop bombs. In wide contrast to this, most Presidents lack the fundamental people skills or creativity to foster lasting peace for a war-torn area. Most Presidents seek importance in terms of historical influence through aggressive action. President Johnson and President G.W. Bush both found out that war has changed since World War II. If a President wants to leave a lasting legacy, facilitating a lasting peace within a war-torn region is the ticket.

If peace is what a President can muster, he would also have to be ok with it when the phenomenal peace that is created makes certain members of the Senate Foreign Intelligence committee or other committees unhappy. I would not think our Senate is capable of doing this, but in the extreme case it is, I will cover the ground. I would hope our Senate would not hold over a President's head risk of impeachment as leverage to help push our nation toward a more aggressive Iranian national security policy. I pray God that our Senators wouldn't even think it. President Trump avoiding war with Iran may also make a handful of American elites that own a lot of oil and refining stocks unhappy. Like Teddy Roosevelt would likely say if he were alive, "Making a handful of men upset is better than hurting America's future and leaving a legacy of death and failure."

The War in Afghanistan & Dealing with The Taliban

The American war in Afghanistan has been going on for 18 years. It seems to me that the nature of warfare has changed, or America would not be having so much difficulty winning wars with its overwhelming firepower. It's not like we have been restricted politically so much in Afghanistan either. The Vietnam war was more political than Afghanistan. The truth of the matter is, you can bomb mountain ranges or jungle into oblivion and it still doesn't really change the landscape by much. Mountains and jungle can absorb a lot of TNT. You just kill the current ranks of young recruits and within 10 years, those ranks are again filled with recruits who want to avenge the deaths of their older brothers and fathers. That's a cycle we really don't want to get caught in with a war. We should know better.

Instead, our challenge with warfare in the 21st century in austere environments such as Afghanistan is to somehow promote peace. *How can we promote an environment where it is beneficial for the government of Afghanistan to police its own?* It is therefore wise that President Trump's administration did conduct talks with the Taliban as a component fostering a potential government within Afghanistan that included representation of the Taliban leadership. Despite all the horrors this faction has been associated with in the recent past, its current leadership is not the same leadership as in the days of September 11th, 2001. I assure you that. Do we want forever war, or do we want peace? That is the question to be had. The Taliban must accept that it does not have authority to control the government of Afghanistan anymore. Rather, it could be an element of the government as representative of its tribal peoples.

Back 40 years ago, elements within the American government were energetically promoting the training and purchase of military equipment and weapons by the Taliban in order to fight the Russians. Back then, we branded the Taliban as freedom fighters and wanted them to cause as much pain for the Russian military as possible. We branded them freedom fighters simply because they were the enemy of our enemy. Unfortunately, Machiavellian strategy doesn't play out in a world where we are now in a global city of sorts. Our nations are too woven together economically for Machiavellian tactics to work well anymore.

Those men that we helped train and obtain weapons trained their sons and grandsons in the use of American fighting tactics. These sons were the ones who accepted a wealthy Saudi man into their midst that was seeking a refuge to establish a powerful kingdom of hate and deceit. The men we trained and helped arm fell prey to the delusion this Saudi man preached, the delusion that a war against America was what God Almighty wanted. This delusion is what led the Taliban to promote the terrorists attacks against the United States on September 11th, 2001. There is no doubt that American clandestine operations helped promote the fertile soil for the Taliban to feel it ruled Afghanistan with an iron rod and could rage war on anyone from its strongholds. American foreign intelligence agencies should own this big fail.

Around the world in the last 70 years, Russia's and the Unites States' extensive use of proxies to conduct lethal operations against their enemies have lost them both the moral high ground to preach at nations like Iran who do the same thing. Our actions in today's world have a higher and higher probability to create unintended consequences because of the interconnectedness of the global community. Raging war on one's enemies through proxy nations or proxy extremists organizations is potentially very hazardous to a nation's goodwill now that the information age is here.

The government of Afghanistan is forever changed, and many of its people have tasted freedom to include freedom of speech and the rights of women to have their own voices and not to be owned or threatened by men. *They are for this new freedom and are not being forced into this freedom by Americans.* The Taliban is delusional if it thinks the old ways can return. However, peace can happen. If the Taliban actually loves their own people, it could swallow the bitter pill of sharing power with other political factions within Afghanistan. Each faction has input that could be valuable for forming a better future for Afghanistan.

The War in Iraq

Simply put, the war with Iraq was a failed geopolitical effort. This war is a perfect example of two strategic realities of our current global economic and political system: First, it shows that the American security apparatus is prone to failure. It has recently made several big miscalculations and apparently can be fooled with false intelligence. Whether this is reflective of our leadership culture having learned the requirement of strong loyalty without dissent from previous generations or simply a national security system related issue, I don't know. Second, it also demonstrates the potential unintended consequences of conducting wars in austere environments or wars that can create unintended political or economic destabilizations.

In short, the potential risks of these effects are likely much higher than previously thought due to our globe now being economically tied together more than ever before. A different type of leader is needed in a more complex world than was needed in the early 20th century. Leaders truly do have to look at the big picture. By leading us into a war in the Middle East shortly after fighting the Taliban, the Saudi man got what he wanted, America to show aggressive tendencies to other nations across the Middle East. Violence spread across the Middle East and America became the center of it. Let's not go to war again in the Middle East based off fast facts that appear out of nowhere.

President G.W. Bush led America into a war that was started by members of his own staff using grossly doctored foreign intelligence reports that were fervently sold to our congressional and military leadership as the real deal. We are later learning that President G.W. Bush potentially had personal beef with Iraq's leadership over what he believed to be a sanctioned attempt on his father's life years earlier. No one could blame him for that. However, it is treading the line of unethical behavior when you convince a nation there is a threat when there is not one. Lots of folks like to run their mouths about just how bad the behavior of President Trump's staff was due to them looking the other way when a foreign government was running online ads to try and influence American votes.

Last I checked Americans had access to thousands of news sources to determine which candidate they wanted to vote for. As far as I know, a foreign power didn't force them to vote for anyone. I'm not saying the behavior is right. However, I would like to contrast this with what occurred with President G.W. Bush's staff. *At the time, our nation's leadership depended on the truthfulness of President G.W. Bush's documents in order to make the proper decision to go to war or not. They did not have many other sources* for this type of information. I would ask those folks that think that some of Trump's election team were involved in the worst behavior ever recorded to rethink their positions.

The Iraq War gained America very little while costing us a lot. It also facilitated a cascading effect that brought strategic instability for the whole of the Middle East. Thousands of Americans and hundreds of thousands of Middle-Easterners lost their lives (some estimates are over a million if you count the spread of violence into Syria and other nations). Because his economic run was overwhelmingly subsidized by government spending without economic policy enhancements, it was a drive that set us up on an unsustainable economic curve which left out lower-income and lower middle-class Americans. They were not able to help the economy out when it began to falter. And, fall hard it did, nearly collapsing the global economy and putting us back into a 1930's style depression.

President G.W. Bush had a way of too heavily trusting the strong men around him for sage advice. Maybe this is ultimately what led to the bad decisions. Our military was already deployed. The experts were saying Iraq could be destroyed and rebuilt within a two to three years. From his own perspective, he was likely just listening to the smart people he hired. All of that advice totally ignored the most important element in nation building. The psychology its people.

President G.W. Bush's team, while of the highest caliber of technical experts in their fields, totally were clueless to the power of people systems that comes from deeply held cultural and religious beliefs. While listening to smart people is good, having the discernment to understand competing priorities and special interests involved is key. A President must also be able to delineate personal feelings from optimum decision making. Only strategic thinking applied in this manner proves viable in the long run. Simply listening to "smart people" and then having smart people make excuses for what they have done after they have created a mess is weak leadership. It's not taking responsibility for the calls you make. Good leaders own their results.

In 2020, we need to reelect a leader for our nation that is blatantly strong yet has the ability to negotiate and compromise in an ongoing manner. We can't afford for our nation to be in gridlock on issues such as gun control, economic policies geared toward helping lower-income and middle-income Americans, or whether or not we should be going to war. The opposite side of the political aisle is not the enemy; it is an opportunity to be capitalized upon for positive change.

Unless it's a fundamental policy flaw such as Reaganomics, compromise is usually needed to achieve meaningful results. You have to look at the other alternatives. President Trump is at least not afraid to make unilateral calls and has the potential to change his mind on key issues, insiders do not. They will follow the party line to the tee.

Turkey's Recent Purchase of Russian Missiles

Turkey has recently (2019), purchased Russian air defense missiles. In response to this, the United States has restricted Turkey's ability to purchase Joint Strike Fighters even though Turkey helped fund the Joint Striker program. I will give the reasons it is understandable that Turkey would want to purchase Russian defense missiles. First off, Russian air defense missile technology is some cases is likely better than American technology.

How we let the Russians with a miniscule budget relative to our defense budget make this stuff better than us is a mystery. They simply must be employing more creative minds. That being said, Turkey wanted the better technology—technology that could actually defend their nation from air attack without breaking its government's budget. It was smart for Turkey to want something better than the JSF to defend its people. That's just smart business not hostile to the United States.

Second, it is well documented that the JSF technology was highly compromised reportedly with China having hacked the files of the JSF program more than 10 years ago. If this is the case, JSF technology is highly compromised abroad and likely easily could be overcome with the right technology. It is no wonder at all why Turkey wants defensive weapons instead of just offensive platforms in order to keep its nation peaceful. What delusions are Pentagon program managers and our nation's highest-ranking defense officials under concerning this? It's no surprise Turkey doesn't want to go all in on a compromised and aged American defense program. Are they lying to our President about this? Have we become filled with ranks of folks at the top in our Defense Department who cannot even think with the level of logic as an average and reasonable person?

The United States should continue to think of Turkey as a major ally in areas such as the War on Terror and other areas where intelligence sharing is helpful. In the recent past, Turkey has been a friend to the United States in many regards even letting the United States utilize its airspace in the first Persian Gulf War. We should re-think consistently playing hardball with nations such as Turkey when we should be building friendships with them. I have gotten to travel to Turkey and speak with ordinary Turkish citizens when I was in the military. They are loving family-oriented people. It's culture and its people are phenomenal.

The Dispute in the South China Sea

The South China Sea is a region with many natural resources at the bottom of the ocean. One of these resources includes "Flammable Ice", a natural resource that is compressed natural gas with up to 20 times the potency of natural gas. Obtaining flammable ice from the bottom of the ocean is a technological challenge; but, for the technology of the future, it may not be. Posturing for being a leader in natural resources of the future as well as keeping trade routes open for its shipping are two major reasons the United States is so heavily involved in territorial disputes going on in the South China Sea. The Unites States has a strong stance against China utilizing atolls or coral reefs as islands and propping these small juts from the sea up by pouring millions of tons of sand around them and reinforcing their structure with reinforced concrete.

This is essentially building artificial islands. By doing this and laying claim to this as actual Chinese territory, China would now control a large amount of territorial waters since these islands would now be considered coastlines. These territories could not be breached by American ships excavating for natural resources or en route to trading partners without permission from China. This would bring greater wealth to China by giving them exclusive claim to the natural resources found beneath the seas within the area. American and authorities are aware of this posturing that is occurring.

Concerning this tension occurring within the South China Sea, I do not have strong opinions on it either way. It is apparent America cannot stop the Chinese government from reinforcing the natural reefs and atolls. The building will likely continue. Ultimately, this will give China an advantage at searching for natural resources as it will be more costly for other nations to search and excavate from shipping alone with no home base for resupply, offload of cargo, or shelter from storms nearby. All I can say is that these natural reefs and atolls are close to China and other nations, not the United States. We've had our many disputes concerning other islands to protect American interests throughout the last 150 years. America has a large footprint internationally concerning territory it considers protectorates that promote its own trade. Us faulting China for doing the same thing close to its own borders is likely very hypocritical in nature. We need to work compromises with China in order to not make an ongoing conflict out of it. We cannot demonize China for doing something we ourselves would likely do if those resources were close to home.

Concerning the element of open trade routes, I think China does have an obligation to grandfather in key trade routes for nations seeking passage through any of these disputed areas. Passage through an area doesn't give permission to excavate an area, it simply means trade routes stay open. China should delineate this and capitulate this allowance for trade as soon as possible via some type of legal international trade treaty.

North & South Korea

All I will say about this region is there is no reason it cannot make peace and move forward in the future. North Korea needs to change its policies if it hopes to be part of the global community. I do not know if America will ever accept a nuclear North Korea in a way that would allow for sanctions to be dropped. It's understandable that the regime fears giving up its nuclear weapons. It believes American and Western powers could then interfere with its current regime. Perhaps legal treaties specifying to the contrary could take this fear away. I don't know. What is for certain, whether North Korea denuclearizes or not, is that a nuclear war isn't going to happen. That's propaganda at it's finest. The only way that would happen is if there were a massive preemptive attack against North Korea and North Korea were able to launch a nuclear response in time against South Korea or Japan. America attacking North Korea for the sole purpose of ridding the world of a dictator with nuclear weapons would in fact be madness. South Korea's economy would be forever damaged by the event and it could potentially cost millions of South Koreans their lives. This is why South Korea recently made it clear to the world it doesn't want war or even the escalation of war.

Mexico

Due to the recent trade war with China, Mexico has now become our largest trading partner according to some sources. Mexico has always been one of our largest trading partners for the last 100 years. To put it simply but bluntly, America is addicted to the cheap labor Mexico provides. "It really isn't in our interest to make them a stable country because then that cheap labor might go away." That's what the American elites believe, not most Americans. We need to be better than this when it comes to standing right by Mexico. We should have been helping Mexico decades ago build a better economy. With all the contributions Mexico contributes to the American economy, why haven't we? As Americans, we should want better for our next-door neighbor than they currently have. We also do not want the flow of drugs crossing our southern borders. The Trump administration is accurate in its depiction and belief that the southern border is potentially a national emergency. However, this emergency can only be eliminated within Mexico not by a wall alone. Better economics that builds Mexico's economy by giving good jobs to the poor is key.

Other Nations of Central and South America

We should consider our side of the globe sacred. The potential for economic growth we could foster with our neighboring economies is massive and there is no need to depend on a few large trading partners if we create a winning strategy of trade with our local nations. America has the right to ensure no undue foreign influence is occurring within our neighboring nations that would lend itself to creating regimes hostile to our own government. Other nations should know that. Even with this being said, America should maintain the moral high ground when it comes to interacting or promoting differing leadership throughout this region.

Unintended consequences can occur when intervening in things such as national elections or local military operations. We intervene most fairly when we shine the light of discovery upon other nations conducting unlawful operations in this region that are contrary to democratic venues for government as well as anti-capitalistic. We do not do well when we attempt covert intervention in elections or conduct lethal operations against foreign leadership. Such operations are internationally considered illegal and attacks on the sacred concept of national sovereignty. We have in times past lost a lot of moral authority due to our conduct in this regard. I would say covert intervention should be a last resort.

The Serious Game of Espionage Between the Great Powers

It is well known that America as well as most other powerful nations such as China, Russia, Britain, France, Israel, Germany, Italy and others have informants and spies embedded in almost every nation on earth, even the nations that are supposed to be their own allies. It is just a sad reality this is how it is. From time to time, some poor American soul is caught up in this game and us general folks back home hear about it on the news as an American that was a student or scientist being accused of being a spy.

Some nations that take this game very seriously routinely conduct purging operations against Western foreign intelligence operations. They arrest who they believe to be informants or spies and sometimes have them killed or imprisoned. The world of espionage is a very sad world indeed. All I can say to all of this is that history should be a teacher to all the relative newcomers of this deadly game. All powerful nations will continue to do this. Russia, Britain, and the United States ultimately figured out in times past that killing each other's informants or spies did little to help stop the game from continuing to be played. Ultimately, they learned to trade back spies creating some form of civility to the game.

Otherwise, killing large numbers of people does considerable damage to the relationship of the participating countries over time and this damage does cause political and economic stressors and conflict. Lowering the lethality of the game is likely in the best interest of all involved. I am not the expert on all of this. What I can say though, is history should be a teacher rather than being disregarded.

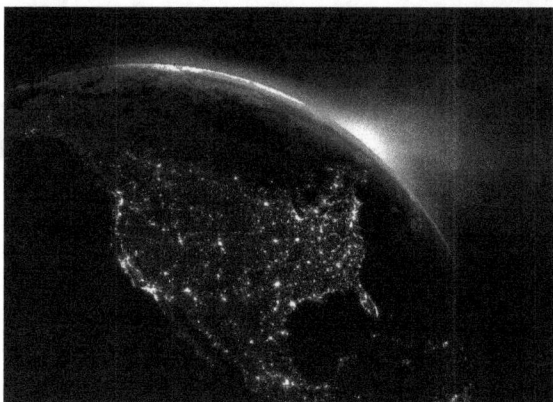

Chapter 9

Immigration Reform & The Wall

It is obvious our Immigration policies in the Unites States need to change. It is not a good or bad, wrong or right issue. Currently, America cannot even sustain its own population without immigration based off our current birthrate. We need immigration. America's growth since its founding was fueled by immigration. The main reason why American talent has been so great throughout the centuries is we have been a melting pot for all different types of people with new ideas who also brought strong work ethic to our shores to fuel development.

Since our early days as a nation, we have greatly changed. Our need to defend our people and borders has also greatly changed. Any scholar trying to sell you something different doesn't understand the reality of today's world. We do need to secure our borders in today's new reality. The wall President Trump partially campaigned on just supports a part of that effort of securing our borders. While it doesn't stop illegal immigration, it helps slow it as well as slow the transport of illegal drugs across our borders. It is a fact that border barriers have been going up in America at an increasing rate for decades. Democrats have heavily supported this changing effort as well . Any arguments that preach against a border barrier are based off the pre-global war on terror era.

One of President G.W. Bush's wisest if not wisest observation was, most Mexican men that were "worth their salt" simply wanted a better life for their families, that's why they would cross the border for a better wage. In many industries, we depended on this migrant labor for over a hundred years. These workers greatly contributed to the American economy and the growth that currently support millions of American jobs. That is a fact. They contributed more than we are now saying they are taking from us in the form of government subsidies. Millions of migrant workers' children were born in America. These children ultimately grew up and culturally, they see themselves as Americans.

They want to continue to live and work and raise families in America. By and large, the great majority of these people are law-abiding family-oriented people. We should think long and hard about their plight prior to raging war on the authenticity of their character and loyalty to America. We really do need to hold ourselves accountable to a Christian way of dealing with this crisis. Strictly from an economic standpoint, we need their labor. We could easily integrate these folks into the American economy and their diversity and talent would make America stronger and a better place to live and work. Republicans should take this issue up with President Trump and encourage a plan to accept American immigrants into our fold that have lived and worked in America for a certain number of years; or, which have parents who have lived and worked in America for a certain number of years. Most could likely prove they have. I would think 10 years is a good number for proving a length of stay and work history, even if that work history was working dozens of odds-and-ins jobs for small businesses who could only afford to pay them under the table.

We also need to be careful when we think we truly know what talent makeup we need for immigrants to most beneficially contribute to the American economy. While I know it is tempting to think we need the most technically talented people from all around the world to immigrate to America, this assumption may be furthest from the truth. I fell for it until I learned more as well. Last I checked, *I thought it was the job of the American education system to create the most talented people in the world so they can acquire high paying jobs.* It is not designed to give the good jobs to immigrants who have not climbed the ladder in America. There are many American mid-grade salary and high-paid hourly workers that have lost jobs in the last twenty years due to tech companies handing the jobs to international employees who obtained work visas.

Our Federal government facilitated the mass distribution of these work visas, especially for tech companies who claim they don't have the talent in America to fill the jobs. Heck, if you really don't have the talent in America for the jobs that are needing filled, create the talent. Work with our universities to create it. It's a sham the way we've funneled such a massive amount of work visas to these large companies only for them to pay the international labor half to three-fourths what they would pay an American.

Plus, these employees are essentially hostages because if they quit, they get kicked out of America. Hey, if I ran a large-scale business and I wanted to cut my cost and raise productivity, I'd want to get as many of these visas as possible! I could take from the American economy and not give back in the form of taxes or American jobs, especially not the good paying clerical or technical jobs! I can internationalize my business and truly elevate my business above the needs of America! That sounds great! On top of that, I will pay myself, the corporate board members, and my most trusted executives millions of dollars to keep all the secrets of how we extract money from America and not give what we truly should be giving back! To put the icing in on the cake, I will donate to a large number of politicians in both major political parties just enough to keep their loyalty! That's a great system!

Instead of this approach, American governmental officials should be taking their oaths of office seriously and putting America first. If we need immigrants to help us with entry level jobs, why are we kicking these immigrants out then allowing for immigrants to come in to take our higher paying ones? This is unamerican behavior. I'm not against giving work visas to immigrants for higher paying American jobs. That's not the point. The point is, legislatively, we should have laws that make that a last resort for companies. Those companies should have to prove they cannot find the applicable talent of an American. When 100 Americans with advanced degrees and certifications apply for a job and the company hires work visa international workers, HR in that company is doing exactly what the President and CEO wants, outsourcing American jobs by bringing in cheap labor.

It's apparent we have issues hiring talent at the lower end of the wage spectrum. All you have to do is go down ay Main Street in America with signs posted that say "Hiring" to see that. Why can't these small businesses get immigrants to work in their businesses? Why are we so prejudiced for the big companies by bringing in highly skilled labor to take away good paying American jobs away from us while we put up roadblocks to small businesses hiring lower paid immigrants? I guess only the big businesses that donate large sums of money to our government get to cash in on the value immigrants can provide to the American economy (at least legally anyways). There are thousands of small businesses that use immigrant labor on the down-low; unfortunately, they can't afford the red tape of getting work visas for immigrants they would like to hire. This is all because our government creates the red tape on purpose around the process where it will be harder for small businesses to successfully navigate through the process. Shame on us. Do you know a few years back, the housing construction industry in America literally was being held back because our contractors simply couldn't find the labor to build American houses? I wonder why? Perhaps the Fed was watching out for its balance sheet that now includes tens of thousands of American homes. It wouldn't want to dilute its equity would it?

That same lack of fluidity in America's current manual labor dynamic is affecting small businesses across America. We should rethink our work visa application process and allow immigrants to apply for a two-year work visa for entry level jobs themselves so long as they have a promised work sponsor affidavit. We should be able to expedite an approval within 30 days for this. The worker would only be allowed to work within a certain wage range during this two-year period in order to ensure businesses are not hiring them for entry level jobs then restructuring their jobs shortly afterwards to take higher paying jobs away from Americans. After two years, the immigrants would be able to climb the ladder just like everyone else. This one policy change could help fuel America's economy for the next ten years. This work visa should also be transferable once by the employee to another entry level job for the remainder of the two-year-period if they find another sponsor. This ensures no abuse of the employee by allowing the employee to find another job if necessary.

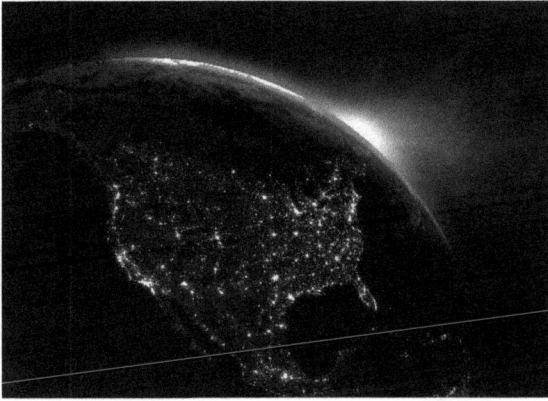

Chapter 10

Abortion: The Reality of Pro-Life & Pro-Choice

Many Americans have strong stances on both sides of the issue concerning abortion. I could show the trendlines concerning abortion over the last 46 years in America. I do not plan to do that. I will discuss a few numbers. The truth is, in most countries, abortion is legal, and an accepted practice used to protect the lives and health of mothers. It is also true that America has a lower abortion rate than many other countries and that rate is at a historic low since abortion became legal. Even so, over the last 46 years in America, 50 to 60 million legal abortions have occurred.

The right to privacy and decision-making authority concerning one's own body is a very strong argument behind why abortions were made legal. Through the power of their votes, American women will likely never again let the legal system determine that right as in times past, women's lives were put in jeopardy during the birthing process through the lack of readily available abortion methods. I understand the *why* concerning the need to let women make their own choices concerning their own bodies when it comes to life and death decisions about letting a pregnancy go on or not. This is the same *why* or *sacred privilege* between a patient and their doctors on many other healthcare issues as well.

As it stands in America now, states are managing the right to have abortions differently. While they are supposed to follow Supreme Court rulings and they do to the letter of the law, they each exercise different legal options in order to make it more or less difficult for women to pursue an abortion. These include adding state level administrative requirements, costs, or by providing resources to make it easier to obtain an abortion. The current as well as the future of American abortion legality hinges on the question of whether or not a woman has the right to abort a viable fetus at different times throughout the pregnancy.

There is not a path forward and there really shouldn't be a path forward with restricting abortions at a level where abortion laws restrict a woman's right to have an abortion to save their own lives, in the event of rape, or in the event the fetus is deemed unviable. That's pretty much a given and even accepted by most social conservatives in America. *The major point of contention then is, at what point, or any point at all does a woman have the right to abort a viable fetus?* It is also understandable that just because the fetus is viable, it does not mean that the pregnancy itself wouldn't pose a grave risk to a particular woman's health. These are the questions currently facing America concerning abortion.

I accept the Supreme Court's rulings on this issue based off the right for a woman's privacy. However, at the same time, I am not a proponent of the abortion of a viable fetus unless the health of the mother is in jeopardy. I do not judge others who may think differently than I do. I believe others should not be condemning each other for differing beliefs. The abortion issue is not as simple of an issue as many folks on either side of this issue make it out to be.   Our knowledge concerning pregnancy and how to protect mothers has greatly increased since 1973.   Back in 1973, I can easily see why the Supreme Court chose the path it did.   Even today, pregnancy is still a very risky event for a woman to go through.

I think it is always a plus when we see women who choose to have their children and give them up for adoption.   In either case, we should make sure women have the option of adoption available to them if we are making sure they have the option for abortion.   If we don't, by de facto action, we are kind of promoting abortion itself because women of lesser means may feel they have no other choice but to get an abortion.   This is especially true in low-income areas where one can rightfully assume that if women do not have access to nearby adoption resources, they are highly likely to seek the only alternative if they believe they cannot support a baby.

As a nation, controlling the scarcity of both abortion and adoption resources should work in tandem with fair and equitable distribution of these resources.   Otherwise, as a nation we are choosing one over the other for specific communities.   If we are doing this, this is discriminatory in the worst of ways.

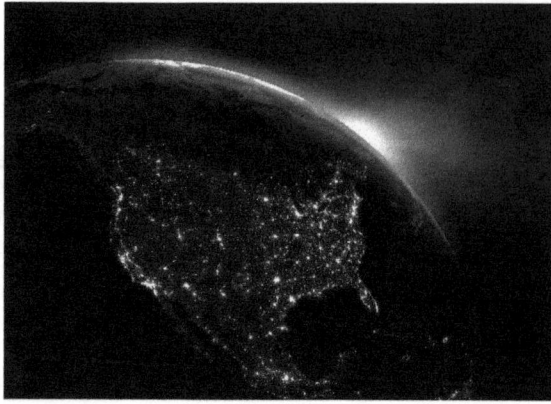

Chapter 11

Equal Opportunity: Citizens' Rights & Education

How is it that in today's America, after all the hardships the civil rights generation, generations of women, and the struggles of LGTBQ Americans and of religious minorities, that Americans cannot treat each other with the respect they each deserve? Whether it be over personal freedom or religious freedom, how is it so difficult to respect another American's personal liberty and right to free will? God made us all with free will. However good intentioned an opinion is, if it is contrary to allowing others to make their own decisions on matters of life, liberty, and the pursuit of happiness, the opinions are contrary to God's intentions for humankind.

Otherwise, we all would have been forced to be compliant to instincts like the animals are. Therefore, the only point of discussion that even should be had is how government should manage the self-evident nature of its citizens' freedoms. Unfortunately, government will never be enough to do this alone.

Citizens must be aware of, and also respect each other's free will within a social and cultural context as well, otherwise, conflict based off meniscal differences in particular interpretations of individual freedoms will continually arise. A good example of this is the recent legal conflicts that have arisen concerning religious business owners that feel they have the right to refuse their services to gay couples getting married. The fact is, they have this right.

In my personal opinion, Jesus wouldn't refuse to do carpentry on the stage of a gay wedding. He probably would be at the reception afterwards drinking with the family and friends discussing his beliefs. That's just my personal opinion though. It's the right of a business owner concerning choices like this not mine. If that's truly how the business owner of a particular faith feels, it is his or her right to refuse service to that customer. Remember though, our government doesn't discriminate on the basis of faith. Therefore, don't complain when someone of another faith refuses a Christian service based off them openly testifying or something causing a disturbance in a business. Things like this can end up flowing both ways.

Getting confrontational or violent about something like this is of a childish nature; especially in a public environment which could embarrass individuals on either side of an opinion. Americans need to turn down the volume on their discontent about someone else or something else. We need to respect each other's personal freedom. Discuss in private or write a personal note about your opinion without finger pointing, threatening, or the use of inflammatory language. This can create a compromise rather than conflict. That usually works a lot better than yelling at them in public or trying to ridicule them throughout the community via the use of online social networks. Doing things like this is just plain childish and smacks of a needy person that wants attention.

Teaching Good Citizenship & Empathy may Now be Required

Since parents have less time to spend with their kids, it would make sense the nation needs to change when it comes to mentoring its young. If a child isn't getting it at home, they need to get the bare minimums at school. You'd be surprised at just how crappy of a job some of our schools do in promoting the maturity of our kids' minds when it comes to citizenship development and civic responsibility. Regurgitating a syllabus without discussion isn't learning. Children should learn the basic elements of the laws they are supposed to follow prior to high school. This includes the responsibility of being a peaceful member of society except in the rare case they are required to use violence for self-defense. They should know the laws so when they are asked to break them, they know better.

This is the type of stuff where our education systems should be teaching ethics and civility at a fundamental level to our children where they can be better than we are today. You would be surprised at just how bad a lot of our kids are concerning impulse control. Another kid offers an opinion on a specific topic to them that they do not agree with and they instantly start verbally attacking the other person or physically slapping or hitting them or something. Little kids are doing this stupid crap.

Many American children lack self-awareness concerning their own emotions and are not checking their behavior when they get angry. Our behavior is within our own control and it has nothing to do with who is truly right or wrong. Mature adults know this. A certain percentage of our kids are not being taught this at home and thus must be taught at school. The only reason these types kids are not dangerous (on average) is because they have never been placed in environments that would make their lack of impulse control dangerous. That's it. They are ticking timebombs. In short, they're brats.

While we've always had brats, it's the brats and angry recluses that grow up and don't have the teachers or parents to regulate their behaviors that we have to worry about now-a-days. Part of education used to be to teach impulse control. To help lower the number of kids who lack impulse control and empathy in our society, our education facilities do not have to preach liberal or conservative values. Instead, it's possible to compensate for a lack of parental guidance at home by instilling common ethics and citizenry virtues within kids at a young age. We need to get some of this going fast for America's schools.

Education that helps kids change their behavior hinges on the education embedding in them both a belief in individual freedom as well as individual responsibility for one's actions. When they have even become a minor scholar on those two things, their behavior changes. Some of our teachers, trusted with the education of our children need to learn these same lessons. That's the portion of the challenge I address at the end of this chapter. If we have teachers with bad attitudes, those attitudes can be transmitted to our children. Some school administrators who hire the teachers don't really understand what their job is either.

We've stopped teaching the liberal arts and social sciences to the point our kids remember these classes for life. Having to be a member of the cast that reenacts a Shakespearean play to one's fellow students or read a portion of a previous famous civil rights speech is powerful stuff. That type of cultural fabric instilled within our children at a young age changes them for the better. STEM successes can best be capitalized on with a culture that can fabricate collectively without undue friction. We need to rethink our course content in elementary, middle, and high schools in order to address the gaps present in the lack of mandatory liberal arts and social sciences education.

It cannot be said enough that these liberal arts and social sciences courses must teach the reasons behind the need for, and the spirit of, civility within our society. Our race to make kids smarter in order not to fall behind other countries in the sciences and mathematics has led us to sacrifice the portion of our kids' educations that helps make them better citizens. We need to fix that fast. When a kid knows that society has come a long way and we are not as bad off as we used to be in most respects relative to a 100-year timeline, their way of thinking changes. We have come a long way and we still have further to go. They must know this at a base level prior to 10th grade if they are going to be a good citizen. They will then be able to use all the knowledge and training of STEM offers in a meaningful and collective manner with their fellow citizens.

The Teacher Protection Society Needs to Change

We hear a lot about how much teachers do with little pay. It's true. I've seen great teachers firsthand do amazing things with kids with little resources. Sometimes, a specific teacher can make all the difference in the world to a specific kid, changing their lives for the better forever. Within some of our communities, we have all the good teachers we need. Unfortunately, in others, we have massive teacher shortages. What the heck is going on?

Across many states, senior administrators who have previously worked as teachers have fostered laws that have created roadblocks to becoming a teacher. It's about protecting their jobs rather than protecting the kids. Did you know that in many states, you could be a top of the line engineer with ten years of experience utilizing mathematics and sciences in world-class companies and it would still take you three years to transition your four-year undergraduate degree into a four-year teaching degree? The red tape school board administrators have allowed state administrators to pass in the name of high-quality education is bogus.

The state-level teacher administration establishment in many states has created a massive amount of administrative and collegiate hurdles in order to be eligible to teach. They'll fill your ears up with things teachers have to know before they are qualified to teach a child. And, at the same time, they'll let classrooms go unfilled with teachers. The teachers holding down the fort within these communities often have up to 40 kids in one classroom. The know-it-all administrators on the school boards and state legislators are dead wrong when it comes to what it takes to be successful in the classroom.

There are many millions of citizens out there that could be put through a one-year teacher transition course and teach any subject needed at the kindergarten through 12th grade levels. Within a year, a program could cover all the essentials such as VARK and the legalities of teacher behavior towards parents and kids. Many of these citizens within a year could be better teachers than a lot of our current teachers. The issue is, a lot of states *don't want it to be easier to become a teacher*. Again, that's administrative red tape designed to protect jobs. This red-tape issue is also tied to the state-level colleges wanting to get bigger and bigger budgets each year. It doesn't take a $100,000 worth of school undergraduate courses to become a teacher at the elementary, middle, or high school levels. Shame on any institution charging that much tuition to a future teacher to get the proper education.

Other college programs in America have become the same way. There is a lot of fluff content within the courses that simply is there to charge more credits and create more cost. A lot of the fluff easily could be taught at the high school levels as well. Instead, administrators make programs that bring the most dollars to the institutions as possible. Vetting our college syllabus content for undue repetitive, fluff, or unneeded course content is key to making our nation's overall education overhead cost leaner. The money comes from somewhere and it is putting a strain on our society. We cannot sustain a nation that charges a teacher the same price for education as it would a specialized engineer considering the higher cost for labs and technical instructors. Charging them the same is darn near criminal behavior by our administrators at the state and university levels.

In times past, if a citizen had enough education and the disposition to teach children (this can easily be screened for), they could teach. No need to get a teaching degree on top of the degree you already have. State Governors could fix the teacher shortage problem in one year across America if they wanted to. If an individual has a related four-year degree from an accredited university, at least three years of experience that includes part-time instructing others such as having had a supervisory role, as well as the patience and moral character to teach children, at maximum it should only take one year to transition this individual to a full-time teaching job in the classroom. With the right full-time transition program, it really could be done in six months.

The only way to change administrative deadlock is with the injection of new talent. If we want talented teachers in the classroom and to prevent teacher shortages, let's make it easier for outstanding citizens to get into the classroom via expedited workforce-to-teacher programs that can transition an individual to becoming a full-time teacher within one year.

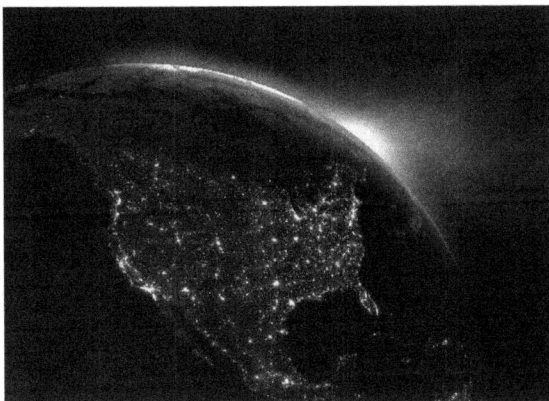

Chapter 12

Legal & Illegal Drug Use & Policy

It's a shame in America we fail to use wisdom in the governance of American health related issues. There is an old adage that goes, "Might makes Right." Well, in America, money is might. It shouldn't be this way on things that truly matter to America's people. At least it shouldn't always be this way. Wealth shouldn't have let the cigarette companies keep advertising for 20 years to our citizens and young people when we knew tobacco was causing broadscale cancer among our population. It did. Wealth shouldn't have let the gas companies continue to sell us leaded gasoline for 20 years when we knew lead was killing our kids. It did as well. Wealth shouldn't have allowed the pharmaceuticals to push pain meds on millions of Americans for long-term use when the pharmaceuticals knew the medications were highly addictive. Wealth did anyways. For all the ills of America, it is still the best thing going. But, we have a long way to go.

Despite all the deaths, alcohol is a part of America's culture and should remain legal. It's up to each and every person to drink responsibility. Alcohol isn't a prescribed drug though. It's a cultural decision. We do a decent job of regulating alcohol, but we can do a much better job of teaching kids the dangers of drinking too much.

On occasion, you see the commercial with a crying parent that is swearing up and down the marijuana led their kids to overdosing on those pills. Really? Have we gotten that attribute in our thinking that we let pharmaceuticals manipulate grieving parents in order to sell us illogical rationale where they can keep the status quo going for the crap that is going on out there today? While in the extreme outlier case, marijuana help lead a kid to his or her own death, this is not the norm. It's the dang pills who killed that child. It is a fact that if the pills never would have been in the house or if only a few tablets would have been prescribed at a time, the kid would not have had the opportunity to steal enough to overdose. How about cigarettes? Have any of our children used a cigarette before getting into pills and then overdosing? Maybe cigarettes are the true gateway drug.

It is sad to consistently watch our federal legislatures buy off on lobbyists' suggestive rationale that is devoid of empirical evidence and deductive reasoning. While marijuana does cause a few dozen deaths in this country annually due to heart complications, driving while under the influence, as well as accidental child consumption of food laced with marijuana, the numbers are very small relative to the number of users. That is a fact.

With the CDC reporting over four million Americans "hooked" on Marijuana and many more millions that use it recreationally each year, statistically, marijuana has to be a very low-risk level indeed relative to other drugs or we would be having overdoses and deaths galore based off the number of people that are using it! For all the talk about marijuana use as a gateway drug and that "it's not harmless", I think we need to rethink what we think is dangerous or not in this country. Almost any food substance including sugar and vitamins can be harmful if too much is taken. Here are some numbers below to consider:

Annual Deaths Caused by Tobacco, Alcohol, Opioids, & Marijuana:

(U.S. 2018 Estimates)

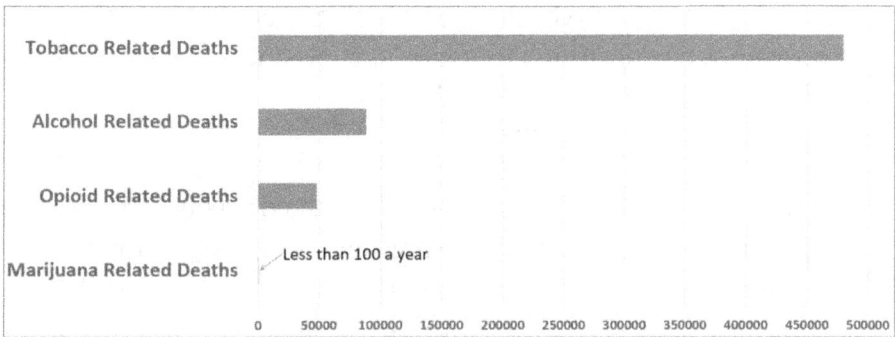

While I am not a proponent of putting any type of smoke into my lungs, I don't hear of people dying from marijuana use on a weekly basis. I do for other types of drugs. Heck, if someone wants to party with friends, what the heck is wrong with marijuana versus people killing themselves with tobacco, alcohol, or opioid addiction? Marijuana is safer than tobacco, alcohol, or prescription pain killers based off statistics. I doubt the average person would be lighting up a joint every day if marijuana was made legal like they do with cigarettes. As far as the potential use for medicinal purposes, it's already scientifically proven that marijuana has the capability to drastically reduce the pain of people in chronic pain without the risk of overdosing and without the risky interaction of chemically made pills.

With opioid pills, our healthcare industry has killed tens of thousands of Americans in the last few years for profit. Shouldn't we change the way we think? We also might want to keep tobacco, alcohol, and pharmaceutical company owners out of the marijuana business because based off their past performance, they would be trying to grow some crazy hybrid plant or sneak highly addictive chemicals into marijuana in order to line their wallets. In other words, our legislatures need to regulate the marijuana industry's type of products appropriately. They would also need to ensure the containers marijuana is sold in are safety sealed to prevent children from gaining access to them. We then would not have to worry about highly addictive variants of plants or children accidentally overdosing from getting into marijuana product containers.

What is likely true is that the tobacco and alcohol companies don't want marijuana to expand its footprint as a party drug because tobacco and alcohol sales might be damaged. Tobacco sales would definitely be hurt. I am not sure about alcohol. Government in America, betrothed to companies such as alcohol and tobacco companies, will need to rethink this arrangement in order to make smarter decisions concerning the safety and health of Americans. I'm not for restricting tobacco, alcohol, or pain pills (when needed). I think Americans should have their freedom. But, if you want to argue marijuana is more dangerous than any of these, you simply are smoking something very strong (and it's not marijuana).

To address another myth fostered by the elite, a person is not a bad person simply because they smoke marijuana. Any Senator that says that is simply someone that's lived behind a white picket fence too long. I don't know many folks myself that smoke or use marijuana. But, the few I know are actually good people. I'd give you the fact that marijuana smells funny. So does cigarette smoke though. The only reason we don't think cigarettes smell as bad as marijuana is because we're so used to smelling it. They both stink.

Restrict both of them from being smoked anywhere where secondhand smoke could be an issue. Otherwise, make them both legal. Marijuana will never cause the public health hazard tobacco causes because people simply aren't going to be smoking or injecting it as much. It can be screened for in drug tests easily. Businesses would still have the right to limit smoking or ingesting it prior to coming to work just like they do with alcohol for public safety reasons. A person that met a certain threshold of intoxication could still be held accountable. America could also make out financially by selling Marijuana legally. The federal government could pay off some of its debt by taxing the heck out of Marijuana sales at a 50% federal sales tax. We could use the money to pay down debt, pay for infrastructure projects, and for education.

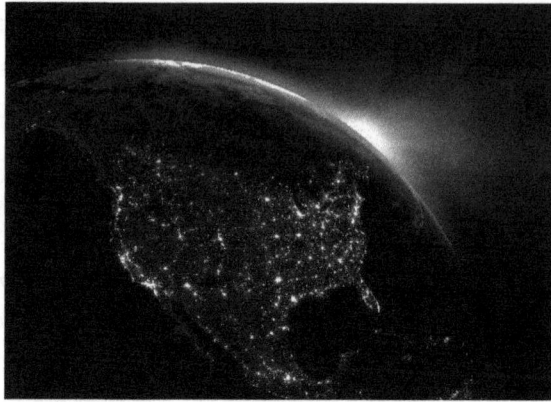

Chapter 13

Protecting the Environment & Climate Change

Domestic and international American capitalism has always been a method that maximizes the use of natural resources and labor. As time has progressed, we've gotten a better understanding about how damaging to the environment we can be with unbridled industrial operations. Running toxic wastewater directly into our lakes, rivers, and oceans used to be just another day in America. We also used to have a lot of smog days throughout big cities in America. Thankfully, those things have improved for all of our benefit due to better legislation at the federal and state levels. We've changed because we've had to change. We started killing ourselves through various forms of higher cancer rates, lung issues, and blood poisoning due to the extent of our domestic pollution. We've figured out it can be bad. That being said, pollution is a natural output of most industrial operations today and we are still far from the zero pollution and carbon footprint type methods envisioned by free thinkers.

Why can't the EPA just do a few things well?

It is understandable why American businesses, for the most part, do not want stricter regulations on carbon emissions. These businesses compete with foreign businesses that have looser controls. This is coupled with the fact that we don't have the very best data yet concerning our emissions' connection to climate change. While climate change is far from being a hoax, we do not understand it in a way that is concrete yet so that leaves the door open for interpretation and our domestic and global business communities will always take advantage of that. We need more complex and accurate models to actually be predictive in nature. Until then, our government and business communities will deny connection based

So, if carbon emission control is an issue that will not be solved by one country or one administration, what should the EPA be focusing on? The bottom line is, Americans need the EPA to do its job concerning key protections against environmental pollutions that effect their lives on a day-to-day basis. If the EPA could just do that well, we all would be grateful. Unfortunately, it doesn't do that well. The rate at which we are continuing to create toxic drinking water supplies in America is getting out of hand. You read about local as well as large-scale companies getting fined for dumping toxins straight into our ground water suppliers ever so often. It seems like we have differing penalties dependent on the state for doing this. In some states, company officials responsible for ordering this done are merely just fined and keep their jobs while in other states, people go to jail. We need to run a tighter ship concerning federal laws that protect our ground water and therefore our drinking water supplies.

Based on the dozens of articles I've read lately concerning current water contaminations issues American communities are experiencing, the EPA is doing a crappy job protecting American water supplies. I don't care if certain elements of water protection are out of the EPA's control. The EPA should still be working with state, local, and private entities to ensure our water sources are being protected. I hope this isn't a surprise to anyone reading this book; but, it's a fact America has toxic levels of chemicals in many of its public water sources that aren't getting any better. In many locations these levels are getting worse. It's a give me that half of the EPA's job should be working with American communities to protect our water supplies. Some of this requires heavy infrastructure investments into our many public drinking water systems at the state and local levels which are aging and bleeding toxins into American drinking water supplies. Our water filters are not getting all this stuff out and we are drinking it.

I challenge the director of the EPA to get an American map, a large one. Put a pin in every location that has had a major (city level or higher) drinking water contamination issue in the last 40 years due to large-scale industrial operations. Are all of these contaminations contained? Do we have public drinking water systems in each of those locations now that are safe to drink? I think not. Roll up your sleeves, call up the Budget Office, and promote federal sponsorships of cleaning up the 100 most vulnerable American neighborhoods that currently have cross contamination of industrial pollutants in these communities' water supplies. Then, help pass legislation in the future that prevents this from happening again and makes companies start footing the bill when it does happen. At the same time, we can put some of the immigrants to work that need legal jobs so they will not be carted off after having lived in America their whole lives.

Another gut instinct I have about the EPA is that it's not doing its job when it comes to protecting America's water reservoirs. Via some type of risk analysis system, have we analyzed the risks to each of our major water reservoirs and do we have prevention plans to help mitigate against contamination as well as reaction plans in place in case they do get contaminated? I doubt it. Why the heck would we not? This is America, we can do better than sit on our hands and wait for a problem to occur. No one should be holding a position of high office in this country that is not trying to maximize their resources to do the best they can to protect Americans and America's future generations.

The Question of Carbon Emissions and Climate Change?

So, the question is, is climate change a hoax? I would say based off the latest data trends, it's not. I am not going to post any of that information. Do I think we understand the true proportion of the contribution humanity is contributing to climate change versus the natural cycles of the earth and sun? No. However, it's not very difficult to understand that in a nearly closed system where you keep contributing certain elements, those elements are going to rise and cause changes. The earth's atmosphere is not completely a closed system due to the loss of some atmosphere continually and creation of different atmosphere continually. *However, it is a semi-closed system.* As we continue to crowd earth in greater and greater numbers, there's no doubt we can begin to cause atmospheric changes based off human activity. In the future, we may be able to compensate for this with carbon air filters. It's a long time until then though. So, I'd say for insurance we should keep a close eye on the numbers.

We take the same approach with large asteroids that come close to earth already. We literally have the technology now to steer an asteroid large enough that could end all life on earth away from impacting the earth. That's freaking awesome. We can protect all of earth's life forms with our knowledge already. There is no reason we shouldn't take other possible disaster scenarios into account as well. Uncontrollable climate change is one of those scenarios. *Only someone totally biased would say to themselves and everyone else, there is no chance this could be happening.* I think the American government should get more involved in the numbers by actually studying the data for themselves in an objective manner and track appropriately, again, for insurance.

Humanity has to realize that we have other cycles such as ice ages and mini-ice ages that naturally occur on this planet as well.

We have to understand climate change in a comprehensive enough manner where we can determine how different input factors interact with each other. How do each of the input factors contribute to the overall output? That's really understanding the data. Natural and man-made forces no doubtable interact as is the case with interactions of multiple factors during production chemical processes.

We have to understand how many natural and man-made forces interact to create a predictive model. I've seen several models of earth's future atmospheric temperatures and they do not all match. With our nation's top scientists, we could easily mathematically model all of this with pretty good confidence levels if we collectively put our minds to it. There are no single correlations that are going to explain it all. We need a more complex, thorough, and accurate climate change model prior to making rash judgements or panic moves.

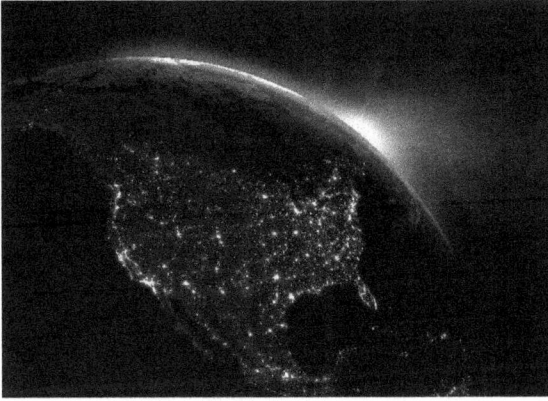

Chapter 14

Minimum Ethical Standards for U.S. Troops

When I was a kid in the 1980's, I met a man us kids at church called, "Brother English." Brother English was in his late sixties when I first met him. He had the old school Marine Corps Eagle Globe and Anchor tattoos as well as many other warfighting tattoos. Some of his tattoos seemed to be out of place in a little country church as they weren't exactly family-friendly. They included faded nudes of shapely women of a bygone era. He obviously was seeking a place in our little church to reflect on his life's many adventures and sins, which he went to the alter almost weekly to seek forgiveness for.

As a Marine in World War II, he was in his twenties, kind of an old man within his infantry platoon. He was the type of guy that would bring candy for all the kids to snack on after church and loved to push the limits of the type of jokes that could be told in the fellowship hall. He could laugh at his own jokes and certainly made a point to laugh at the pastor's and other Brothers' jokes no matter how unfunny Christian humor could get. He also had the ability to make coins disappear and match sticks move all by themselves and all the kids thought that was amazing. It took years before we were able to coax out of him how he did his magic.

He learned this stuff on the way to the Pacific theater while on naval vessels with his fellow Marines and Sailors. He also had picked up the habit of smoking heavily while in the Marine Corps and that gave him his barrel-chested voice along with a case of emphysema he fought the last 10 years of his life. In either case, I knew Brother English for about 10 years at the end of his life as a kid. When I got a little older, he found out that I might want to be a military pilot. I also had begun to read up on military history and had begun asking him questions about the Pacific Islands campaign he had fought in. I was awed when he showed me the scars in his back and stomach from shrapnel wounds. His torso was a mangled mess. Some of the shrapnel was still in his body which his wife attested to. One of his buddies had also been bayoneted to death right next to him by a Japanese soldier. He was so close that the bayonet went through the body of his buddy and just slightly pierce his own abdomen. His buddy died but he survived after killing the Japanese soldier.

Toward the end of his life, Brother English let me know that his nickname back in the Corps was "Little Joe." Little Joe had certainly been in the thick of the ground fighting that occurred in the Pacific Islands. He lived through several beach landings and subsequent occupations by Marine Corps and Naval forces. During some of his time in the Pacific, some Marine rifle squads were tasked to fan out and cover all possible island territories where enemy soldiers could still be hiding or taking up fighting positions against Americans. It was a dirty side of the war because on some of the islands, the Japanese literally fought to the death.

Some Japanese ground forces brainwashed the local civilians into believing there was no hope to surrender with the Americans. They were told fighting Americans to their deaths was the only honorable thing to do. While many Japanese civilians did surrender, some of the civilian men were seen as possible spies or willing workforce of the Japanese Army, so they were not treated well by the Marines. In the chaos of the fighting, it was understandable that hundreds and perhaps thousands of Japanese civilian men, woman, and children were shot.

If that were the whole story, I think Little Joe could have stomached it without having to go to the alter weekly toward the latter portion of his life. Bad stuff happens in war. And in the chaos of fighting, Soldiers and Marines will kill on the drop of a hat when rounds are coming at them from all different directions. That's a given. *Sometimes, warriors go beyond this though and kill when they know they should not.* Sometimes warriors depart because of the fear and anger that turns them against the civilization of another type of people altogether. This has happened throughout history and in every war, it at least happens on a microscale. Thankfully, not so much on mass scale anymore.

That morning, Little Joe had been asked to stick close by the side of his Marine Squad's Sergeant (the Squad Leader) on the patrol they were conducting. Their platoon had been shot up during the beach landing just a couple weeks prior and the previous squad leader had been killed. This squad leader was meaner and tougher. His promise was to do his best to get them all home alive. Little Joe and all the guys respected him greatly. This Sergeant trusted Little Joe to be his number-two guy, to have his back. No one messes with a Marine Corps Squad Leader in wartime, period.

Little Joe's squad along with many other squads of Marines were having to clean up the rest of the island. Everyone was afraid of being bayoneted to death or beheaded by a Japanese soldier with a sword jumping out of the brush. So, everyone was tasked with being on high alert on this patrol. After a couple hours, the squad found a small clearing with a Japanese make-shift hut in it. Several Japanese women with small children had come out of the hut and were in a circle hugging each other. The Squad Leader and Little Joe were summoned to take a look. The Squad Leader and Little Joe approached the women and children within about five yards range.

Little Joe had thought his Squad Leader was going to try to offer these women food or water for their kids or something. However, he knew different when his Sergeant raised his submachine gun and took aim. Little Joe was in shock. His Squad Leader paused for a second like he was having second thoughts. It was during this pause that Little Joe was about to say something to him, his words were on the tip of his tongue when the Sergeant opened fire. The Sergeant methodically fired in short bursts like he had been trained to do until he killed about a dozen Japanese woman and children. This happened within about 10 seconds as the Marine squad stood and watched. Afterwards, Little Joe still in shock was able to muster the words to say to his Sergeant, "Why'd you do that?" The Sergeant responded in a belligerent manner, "Because if our father's had done that 20 years ago, we wouldn't be fighting this war now!"

Brother English told me this story when I was just a young man. It left a mark on me because it had left a mark on him. There's no doubt the story is true. He wasn't against me joining the military. I ended up being a Marine like Little Joe had been. What he wanted me to know is that in the military, I might one day have to choose to do the right thing. He told me he wished he could have done something differently that day to make things turn out differently. He wasn't the one who pulled the trigger killing those innocent Japanese civilians; but, he lived a lifetime afterwards with regret that he hadn't stopped it. He didn't have a lot of time to make a decisive decision to challenge his Squad Leader. The fog of war had made the rules unclear in all the crazy fighting going on at the time. Nobody was keeping score. The Marines that participated in the fighting were just glad to survive and make it home. No one was reporting the killing of innocent Japanese due to the suffering they had brought onto our nation. During the later portion of his life, I'm pretty sure Little Joe had several conversations with God about it down at the alter on Sunday mornings. He'd occasionally cry right down at the alter and us kids didn't understand how such a tough guy would do that.

In Iraq in 2005, my helicopter squadron flew Marines and Soldiers around to the point of their intended targets and they would conduct the tough work of clearing houses searching for insurgents and weapons caches. Afterwards, they would bring enemy prisoners of war (EPW's) aboard our helicopters for transport. We would either drop them back at the airbase prison or at the Abu Ghraib prison. At the time, we had no clue all the games and torture that was being invoked on these EPW's inside the Abu Ghraib prison by a small element of senior governmental representatives and soldiers. At least the Airwing mid-level officers didn't know.

What I can say is, most Soldiers, Marines, and Sailors wouldn't have approved of it. I was in the military long enough during a wartime period and I personally knew hundreds of Marines, Soldiers, and Sailors. I can tell you that the conventional forces by and large would not have approved of it. No matter the tough characters you sometimes get throughout the military culture, a great majority would have shunned the use of torture. And, whatever crapload of labels our government wants to throw on enemy fighters in the Middle East, the bulk of them are soldiers, not terrorists, despite what our intelligence community might want to sell Americans (not all but most are). We need to respect them as such, or our own troops have zero chance of being respected if captured.

A small city named Haditha in northern Iraq has a large strategic site known for a dam called the Haditha Dam. I offloaded onto it several times and did other operations near Haditha from time to time. Shortly after I got back from Iraq in 2005, this area made headlines with a Marine platoon getting into trouble there due to a situation that turned out to be similar to what Little Joe went through in World War II. A lot of careers were affected. I remember back in the U.S. a couple of years afterwards; I attended a Marine Corps social where some of us knew the other officers and Marines caught up in the Haditha mess. I can tell you firsthand, these guys were not deemed of clean status by their fellow Marines.

Outsiders who look on the military sometimes get the view of what happens after scandals such as Haditha Dam all wrong.

Yeah, there was a coverup, and yes, some Marines departed from our known rules of engagement of war. But, that doesn't mean the actions of these Marines represent what the Marine Corps as a whole stands for. No matter if it was during World War II in 1943, or if it was during Iraq in 2005, Soldiers and Marines know the rules. They go outside of the rules for the most part due to a temporary break in mental discipline that potentially could happen to any of us when killing others has become the norm. Our training failed them.

We have to inject ethics more deeply into our warrior training. I know prior to going to Iraq in 2005, I did receive ethics training that was pushed by Congresswoman Nancy Pelosi and others. I will give her credit for that as well as having the sense to oppose destabilizing the region in the first place. However, a lot of our warriors such as special forces at the tip of the spear cycle through warzones continually. They therefore should be continually reminded of their ethical obligations as representatives of our great country.

As a country, we either cherish the moral high ground during the conduct of war, or we do not. There is not a lot of gray area here. Of course, as I mentioned before, in the heat of battle, things happen. That's a given. But, there's a big difference between shots fired in an outie or hasty way causing collateral damage and the cold-blooded killings of innocent civilians. It's insanity to think otherwise. And, I'll remind my fellow Americans it sure the heck isn't Judeo-Christian in any fashion.

One of the recruitment posters of World War II showed a drawing of an American man tearing off his suit in order to put on a fighting uniform. On the poster is read , "Germans kill women and children." This angered the American man enough that he wanted to go to war to fight for what was right, to protect the innocent. What we represent as a country matters greatly for the future of mankind. It's not what we say that speaks volumes. It's what we do.

I am not naïve enough that I would think that in the shadows, where our intelligence communities operate and in extreme cases during war, torture or the killing of civilians is never authorized. I would say this to that reality. There is a reason this stuff happens in the shadows. We have been ashamed of it even in the medieval ages. Even the powerful Kings of old wanted to be seen as just in the way they yielded their power. The appearance of unjust authority weakened their position politically and it empowered their opponents at home and abroad. In the information age where history records events and distributes them globally in seconds, how much more does leadership need to keep its nose clean?

A society's goodwill is a powerful building force. An America that authorizes torture and kills unarmed civilians regularly will not be an America that is strong in 100 years. Its own people will stop believing in it. The government will ultimately have to run the country without the buy in of its people and that greatly weakens a nation. America can never stand in the light by being a country that gets its hands dirty on large scale with this stuff. Even simply limiting this argument to the value of the moral high ground in relation to economic growth, righteousness of a nation matters. My point here is not about the mistakes as a country we've made. Almost every country makes mistakes. It's about what we are doing now, moving forward for the reputation of America. In Judeo-Christian culture, the only way to do that is to own those mistakes and promote a higher level of virtue for ourselves in the future.

"But Torture gives us Meaningful Intelligence"

It's always a wonder to me when working in manufacturing, a small group of very experienced and knowledgeable employees that want to improve their machine will make a big change then come back joyfully showing the positive results. They will show trend charts with their machine's performance, "Look, we get a lot better results." Perhaps they save 15% a year creating a million dollars' worth of savings. Ultimately, the way they ran the machine though caused the machine to die three years early creating the need to buy a new machine three years early. Their actions ended up costing the company an extra five million dollars during a budget year in which the machine purchase was not planned.

The employees that caused the mess retired recently so there is no one to blame. The business just has to absorb the extra cost due to short-sightedness. Or, in other cases, their changed method pushed more cost to another area of the facility negating any savings they created altogether in real time. This happens all the time in the business world. Unfortunately, this tactical way of thinking happens on our battlefields and in our government chambers as well. "We know the intelligence gained from this individual saved ten American lives!" "Maybe it could have saved hundreds!"

The problem with this way of thinking is, it's tactical or operational level thinking at best. These type of actions by America are the very cannon fodder that terrorists use in their recruitment videos and manifestos. Nations can ultimately have to fight whole wars in the future based off losses of their moral high ground. Losing the moral high ground can also cost a nation allies, which share some of the casualties incurred during battle and the economic burden of war. Whatever America thinks it is gaining by openly approving torture, it's losing ten times the amount in my opinion in its goodwill reservoir. And, I assure you our goodwill reservoir is valuable, it saves lives and it helps create massive ongoing prosperity for future generations. President Trump, Senators and Representatives: America needs to change in this respect. Our children and grandchildren should not have to look back and correct our mistakes or be ashamed of who we were.

For the Soldiers, Marines, and Sailors who have departed from the path they know is right, just like Little Joe had to do, there are alters all over America that you can go to, to speak with your maker. One thing American culture has that other cultures lack so much of is, a belief in redemption. Like Little Joe, a warrior has to recognize a wrong has happened in order to make it right. It's not fun to have to look within and know you departed from the straight and narrow. We all have. However, when what you've done has caused the unneeded destruction of God's creation, there's a costly damage that occurs to the soul for that. Only a warrior in that situation can take responsibility and make the climb back up from that fall. No one else can do it for him.

President Trump and the Protection of Warriors

After all of that some folks might think I'm upset with the few times President Trump has stuck his neck out to support a warrior that has departed from the straight path. That would be an incorrect assumption. As far as I know, the President isn't pardoning warriors left and right who have killed innocents or noncombatants. He has however, occasionally used his influence to support keeping them out of prison for the rest of their lives. Concerning his actions, I would like to put it this way to our U.S. Representatives.

When a warrior kills outside of mission requirements for the gratification of ego, for anger, or for sport, 99% of the time he lost his moral compass somewhere in combat. In simple terms, he's lost it. There's a mental capacity to war and some warriors temporarily break down. As a nation, we are not injecting deep enough ethics into our warrior codes. In part, it is no doubt our legislatures' fault. We need better oversight of our "tip of the spear" warrior ethics training. I am not justifying the murder of innocents. To the contrary.

Our legislatures and commanders of our combat arms communities need to take responsibility if we are going to lower the rates of these incidents. Simply saying these warriors knew the rules and it's all their fault is crap. We aren't instilling the right values because we are afraid of making a weak warrior. That's a fact. And, that reason is hogwash especially in today's age. A system where everybody knows the rules and can be held accountable is the only way to control our elite warriors' behavior. Warriors must hold other warriors in check for ethical behavior on the battlefield. That is the only way.

A President taking up for a warrior that has departed from the path in order to prevent him from spending the rest of his life in prison is not unbecoming of a President. It is actually empathetic behavior because it acknowledges that we all bear the responsibility of warrior management, not just the warrior himself. We must be better as a society. When a warrior kills routinely, this killing can become trivial and routine in his mind. The only thing that counters that are warrior codes that make it dishonorable to knowingly do these things. At this point in time, we are not managing our warriors appropriately.

A President preventing a nation from having a scapegoat is actually a good thing. We all bear responsibility with a warrior that has fallen from grace. We need to fix this as a country. We need better escalation of force and ethics training especially for our elite warriors. We need it fabricated into their code concerning the protection of innocents. And, it needs to be ongoing, not just once at the start of their careers.

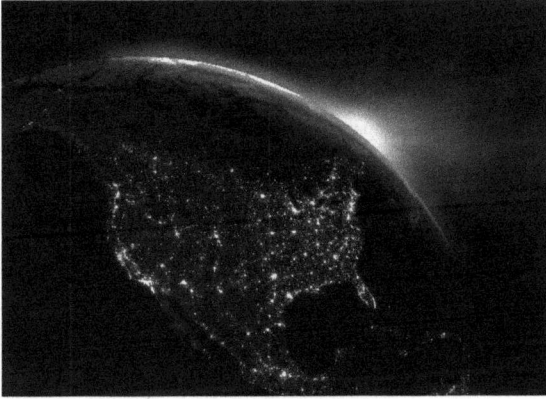

PART IV

Our Future Potential

"The Game's not Over til it's Over."

-Yogi Berra and Red Holzman
(Both are credited with versions of this in Sep and Oct 1973 respectively)

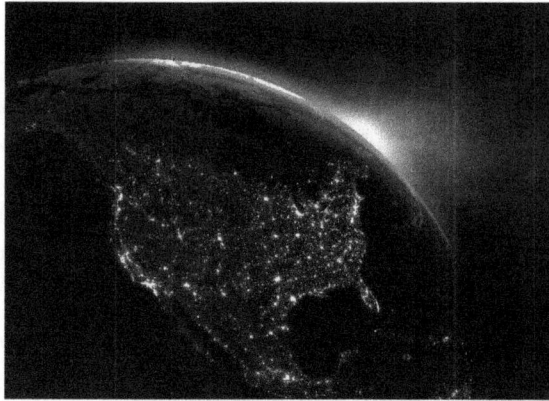

Chapter 15

Trade Agreements & Partnerships

When the National Security Act of 1947 was completed, it arranged the American government into pillars that remain today. While we have created new departments such as the Department of Homeland Security since then, the post-World War II government still resembles our government we have in place today. America was positioned at the end of World War II to be the breadbasket of the world since Europe and Japan's economies were severely damaged due to all the bombing that had occurred. America along with the Russia quickly got to work supporting the economic growth of countries aligned with their own political ideologies. The world's economies grew rapidly. From 1947 to 2018, the world's competing economies also swapped positions concerning placement at the top. As seen on the next page, the world's economic picture as of 2018 was very different than it was in 1947:

The Size of The Top Ten Real GDPs 1947 versus 2018

(In Trillions USD, Adjusted to 2018 Dollars)

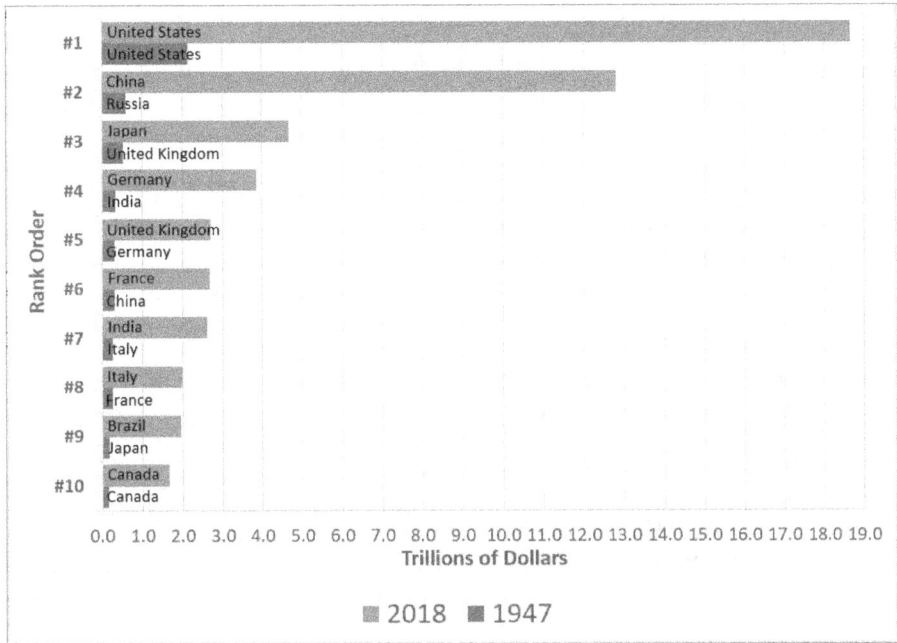

The secret behind all the economic growth was international trade. National economies benefit from trade primarily for two reasons. Number one is that depending on a country's labor force, natural resources, and resource transportation costs, it may be able to produce certain products much cheaper than another country. Therefore, swapping products naturally makes both countries richer in total products. Number two is even if a country can make certain products cheaper, it may need to use its production capacity for what it deems are higher priority products.

In this case, it is still cheaper overall in the form of value to the country to buy the products from another country. In both cases, both countries that swap products become richer. There are many other reasons countries benefit from trade. I'm not an economist but the previous two reasons I just mentioned are reason enough to remember that free trade works.

The world's trade opportunities are not the same as they were in 1947. We cannot hold onto the trade alliances of 1947 and believe they will protect our economic future. While we still can be supportive of our allies who have been with us over the last 105 years militarily, we have to continually make new trade partnerships that reflect the needs of our economy in order to do what's right for the American people. America should be building a broad trade coalition of a Top 100 Trading Partners into our international trading strategy in order to introduce the power of redundancy and diversity into our economic system. There are certain qualities to quantities in and of themselves when it comes to system strength. Ever hear of the single-point-of-failure concept so prevalent in many of our technological devices and software applications today? Well, that tactical system concept is very applicable in the strategic realm of international trade as well.

President Trump's trade policies have attempted to shake up the current economic order to create better advantages for American trade. Previous setups were not conducive to continued wealth accumulation for the average American. Combined with changes in trade policies, domestic business management policies must also be changes in order to benefit Americans' wallets. With all the increase in wealth due to trade over the last 72 years, many Americans have not reaped any of the benefit in real wage growth. This is in part due to our government allowing large companies to sit on massive piles of cash they extracted from the use of overseas labor while using our roads, schools, and conducive business growth environment in the United States to headquarter their operations. While doing so, they avoided paying taxes through loopholes. They also imported cheaper labor to take higher-paying jobs from young salaried workers and higher paid hourly technical workers. They became free riders on the system. The large companies such as tech companies literally have stolen trillions from America proper. We've let them do it. Now, they sit on huge piles of stolen cash and threaten not to reinvest it to aid in supporting American growth unless they get the policies they want passed in our state and federal legislatures.

President Trump has been addressing some of this behavior with our large monopolistic companies. We need strong legislation to discourage behavior like this or we'll never get the reinvestment back into America from freed trade that we should be getting. Restricting incentives to large companies who export our jobs and import cheaper labor for our better jobs, is a start. Restricting any federal, state, and local tax incentives or grants to companies who meet the criteria for this behavior will help even more. Federal law could restrict states from giving tax shelters to companies that participate in this behavior.

Governors are desperate to bring jobs to their states so the restriction of incentives to monopolistic companies must be done at the federal level for companies not to be able to pit state against state to get what they want. A broad coalition of free and fair trade combined with strong domestic policies that protect the American worker will raise Americans' standards of living and support stronger economic growth for America in the coming years. This will stop the large multi-national conglomerates that call themselves American companies from preying off America's workers and America's infrastructure while hoarding U.S. dollars.

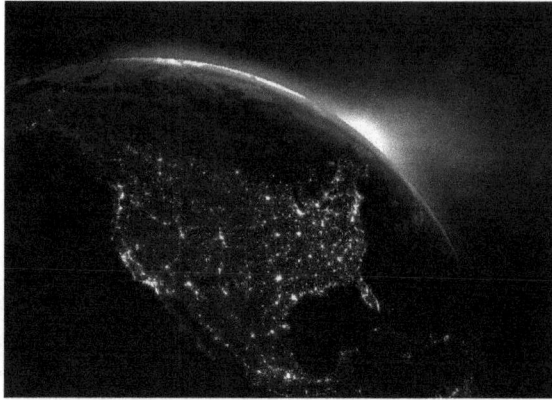

Chapter 16

The Pursuit of Technology:

Energy, Artificial Intelligence & The Space Program

The Race for Energy Dominance

The Race for energy dominance has been ongoing for the last 75 years as America has depleted its oil supplies. In the last 20 years, America has become more energy dependent taking some strain off its oil-dominated foreign policy which is in the benefit of all. In the next 75 years it is possible that other forms of energy such as "flammable ice," which is so prevalent in the South China Sea, could become just as sought after as oil. While it is not likely that any form of natural resource will take the place of oil as king of substrates for plastic products, it is highly likely oil could be replaced by other natural resources for energy creation.

Oil as an energy source is already being replaced by renewable energy resources and natural gas. What can be said is that the world still is not currently short of oil supplies so oil will remain important to the global economy for at least the next 50 years.   Iranian oils supplies should be considered sacred for promotion of global growth in the next 50 years.   Bombing Iran into oblivion would ultimately hurt global growth as an insurgency could potentially sabotage or make too expensive any hope for foreign powers to extrude oil from its territory.   It is better to facilitate international trade in a way conducive to global growth rather than constrict oil supplies in hopes for regional energy dominance.

Artificial Intelligence

Artificial intelligence can be used for thousands of applications in areas such as education, commerce, health, infrastructure, natural resource conservation, agriculture, space exploration, and in general human experience and development. We should be focusing the use of artificial intelligence in functional areas such as these instead of spy games. While our government will have to protect its citizens with the use of artificial intelligence (fighting fire with fire), the focus of its use should be in other areas that support nation building and economic growth.

Businesses and governments already use advanced software programs to analyze data and patterns in way to create valuable information. Combined with this ability, monitoring techniques are used that utilize a customer's data and preferences to capitalize on evaluating each consumer's needs and wants. This advance ability to monitor and analyze is helping guide the decision making of businesses and governments across the globe as well as providing for tailored customer experiences. This ability is here to stay and will only get more advanced.

Businesses and governments have been using the analysis of information for a long time to drive their operations. The latest methods that use technology to heighten the capture and analysis of customers' or citizens' (or foreign citizens') behaviors and preferences is nothing new. The power of it all is just multiplied by the latest technology able to streamline and screen information. The American Supreme Court has confirmed through several rulings that

American citizens' rights to privacy is assumed within the U.S. Constitution. Thus, the footprint of both business and government "big brother" operations should be legislatively required to respect those Supreme Court rulings except in the case of extreme necessity as outlined by American law. Breaches of privacy in America should be harshly punished if we are going to maintain a free society.

There are other applications of artificial intelligence that can allow for independent operating machines or devices to participate in the capture of information, sabotage, or even lethal operations. The age of these devices is already here no doubt and is here to stay. We can only imagine what is already out there. Governments, political opponents, and even some businesses around the world already use these devices for monitoring. Ultimately, the American government has the same responsibility to protect its people from the use of these devices as it does against "big brother" monitoring occurring through the capture and analysis of data through the internet. Once proof of illegal monitoring has occurred, the penalties should be harsh enough to deter future use.

The Space Program

Most Americans support our space program and are willing to continue expending a significant portion of American taxes to support it. The technologies developed within the space program have been shown to improve the lives of Americans. However, in the past, our program has been heavily connected to military technology. We should more handily desynch the two sides of our space program. With NASA working with civilian space companies, America should already have had a successful manned mission to Mars. Just as Kennedy did in the 1960's, it takes the American President setting concrete goals to challenge our large bureaucracies to move forward.

While I'm not a believer in rampant life among the stars, I do believe it is the destiny of human civilization to expand its footprint beyond earth. Ultimately, human civilization could become life among the stars. Even with our current technology, we know that we can capture the momentum of photons with a light sail and project small objects to a high rate of speed, potentially up to a third or more of the speed of light. It is just a matter of time before the United States, a large corporation, or another country captures this technology in a way to start using it. America should be at the forefront of the utilization of fractional-light-speed travel for both military and civilian functions. This is the future any way we want to slice it. I would hope we capitalize on it in the civilian realm in a much greater way than the military realm.

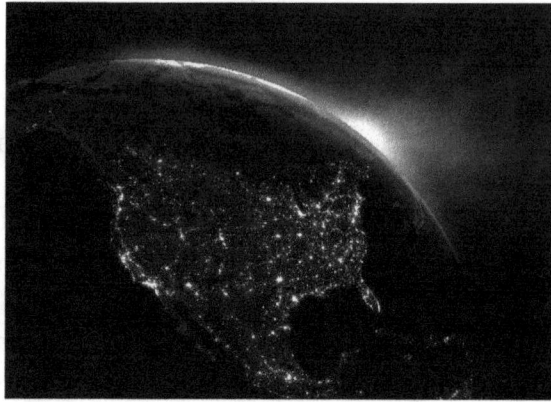

Chapter 17

Establishing America's Long-Term Health
Summary of Top 20 Recommendations to our
Legislative, Judicial & Executive Branches

Throughout this book are recommendations through which the United States could improve the future for its people and its government. If implemented, the recommendations would help support continued economic growth and better lives for millions of Americans while creating a more sustainable economic system. America is meant to continue to lead the world by possessing the moral high ground politically, economically, and militarily.

To make that a reality, our leadership must have more courage and be resolved to stand for fundamental virtues that don't payout overnight. Those virtues, like seeds, take time to grow. The primary issue concerning America's growth is the courage of its leadership to face special interest groups and the ultra-wealthy with the need for change. The secondary issue is simply the work ethic to roll up their sleeves and do the hard work necessary to create phenomenal legislation. When's the last time our legislatures worked 48 hours straight to contribute to something good? And then, turn around and did it again a few times a month for a couple of years? Why wouldn't they be willing to work this hard to contribute to the future of the greatest country on earth? Instead of having the faith, courage, and work ethic to lead us to better things, they are letting an insufficient push system of economics stand because it's just too damn hard to do the right thing. This system is leaving 50% of Americans behind. We can fix this if we're strong and willing to work together. We can build a better America for our kids and grandkids to live and work:

ACTION	U.S. President	U.S. Senate	U.S. Representatives	SCOTUS	Federal Agencies	Governors & State Governments	CEO's & Corporations
#1 Prioritize a broad coalition of trading partners (A Top 100 List) and develop trading partnerships with each. Trade coalitions can account for some of the Top 100. However, all trading partners are important in order to maintain a diverse and adapatable economy.	X	X	X		X	X	
#2 Develop robust federal and State Laws to regualte special interest groups. Better regulate interactions and contributions to federal and State legislation.	X	X	X		X	X	
#3 Depolitisize the federal minimum wage by formulizing it.	X	X	X		X		
#4 Track federal and State spending by the 8 categories mentioned in this book. Trend GDP percentile spending in this way and compare backwards for 50 years.	X	X	X		X		
#5 Spend more wisely in all categories but especially in the Keeping Us Safe category where so much waste has occurred with marginal value which has not actually kept Americans safe in the last 40 years.	X	X	X		X		
#6 Invest more into our Infrastructure, Education, and Commerce categories.	X	X	X		X		
#7 Rebuild a comprehensive space program with big milestone challenges set for us as a nation. The program should benefit both civilain and military applications but with a focus on civilian application.	X	X	X		X		
#8 Regulate healthcare providers and pharmecueticals in a way that prevents regional monopolies, price fixing, and the unnessesary over prescription of opioids.	X	X	X		X		
#9 Provide a fallback national healthcare insurance plan for Americans that prevents States from taking advantage of their citizens in need.	X	X	X		X		
#10 Embrace the LLORD system or similar systems of giving back to American communities that disperse the good to grow the good as rapidly as possible.							X

ACTION	U.S. President	U.S. Senate	U.S. Representatives	SCOTUS	Federal Agencies	Governors & State Governments	CEO's & Corporations
#11 Stop the flow of campaign funds across State lines creating a lack of civility in State and local elections. Campaign funds should be raised within the State by State citizens. Corporations should have the approval of all corporate members including their employees prior to giving any money in the name of the corporation.	X	X	X	X	X	X	X
#12 Provide more qualifying events for parents to take time off to be there for their kids without penalty from work. This should include an expansion of federal legislation that allows a Mom or Dad to take a discretionary two weeks unpaid time off to focus on family for other reasons besides emergencies without fear of job loss.	X	X	X		X	X	X
#13 Track total hours worked per household as a balancing metric against total household income per household in order to see true household wage per hour worked. This can tell you in good or bad economic cycles the bardering power of a parent's time at any specific income bracket. This affects quality of life for Americans.	X	X	X		X	X	
#14 Pass sensible gun control laws that do not try and confiscate guns from Americans. The legislation should focus on high-capacity magazines, background checks, and a requirement to document all gun sales and transfers moving forward without loopholes.	X	X	X		X	X	
#15 Avoid preemptive war with Iran so long as Iran is not attacking Americans or our Allies in a way to create large scale casulties. Respond in kind to any escalations of force. Seek to make Iran an ally in the GWOT with Iran helping to quell terror organizations.	X	X	X				
#16 Promote deeper friendships with neutral countries such as Turkey. Do not try and pitch Turkey against Russia, China, or Iran.	X	X	X				
#17 Pass legislation that keeps higher paying American jobs from being given away to work visa holders unless a company can prove Americans are not available. Promote lower paying entry level jobs be given to immigrants through work visas. Allow immigrants to work their way up. Small and large businesses would benefit.	X	X	X				
#18 Fix the teacher shortage by making it easier to transfer a 4-year degree into a teaching degree. Remove State laws that make unnecessary hurdles to becoming a teacher so long as the candidate possesses the accredited credentials and moral character.	X	X	X		X	X	
#19 Protect American water systems and resevoirs. Fund grants to heavily support water system upgrades. Hold businesses accountable for illegal dumping into our water supplies and recover damages to the environment with lawsuits and executive actions capable of freezing business and personal bank accounts.	X	X	X		X		
#20 Ban the use of torture unless approved by the U.S. President in the extremely rare case mass casualties could occur if not used. Embed in our warrior codes the responsibility to protect the lives of innocents if mission allows for it. Require warriors to check other warriors' behavior.	X	X	X		X		

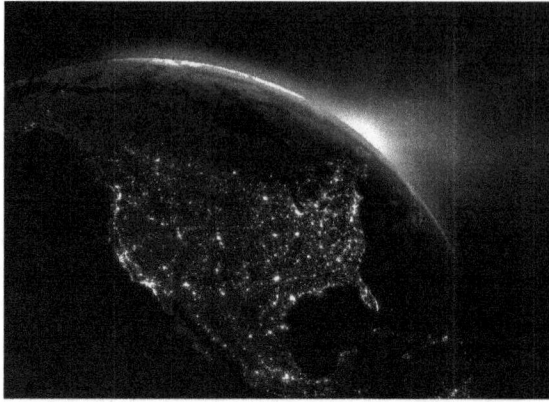

Chapter 18

A New Letter to President Trump

Writing a new letter to the current President of the United States is intimidating. He doesn't know me from Adam, so I have no idea if he'll receive the message or not. In either case, if I were to have the ear of the President for a few moments, I would say the following on behalf of the 50% of Americans who really have been left behind in the last 40 years:

To the President of the United States of America, President Trump,

Congratulations on your successes during your first term in office. Even with a flourishing economy, there are a lot of underlying political and cultural tensions in play throughout American communities right now. Part of the reason why I wrote this book is to help show there are economic reasons for much of this conflict and it's not just about the political and cultural differences both sides' ideologues push. I hope you can overlook the small inaccuracies pundits may find with the data in this book and see through to the spirit of the book's analysis. I believe it paints an accurate picture of the current challenges America is facing. I did my best with creating an accurate data-based analysis of ongoing issues that matter to Americans, though I did work with limited resources. My wish is that your administration and future administrations can use this book as a resource to promote healthy growth of the American way-of-life for the decades to come.

If elected to a second term, my hope is that you would buck convention and fight to resolve current conflicts dividing Americans. I would think you'll have to wrestle with your own political party to come together with Democrats to create win-wins. Being willing to challenge convention and fight for something new is one of your greatest strengths. That's huge to have in the office of the Presidency right now. Your ability to change your mind quickly is a strength that scares some elites at the top. But, that ability may be the fuel we need as a nation for economic change that would benefit both liberals and conservatives in the coming years. Teddy Roosevelt had to fight pretty hard for Americans about 115 years ago. It was only by shear fate that America ended up with this guy in the oval office. Without him, America would have never become a place where people from all around the world want to come and work. I think it's time for another President to take some actions on behalf of the American people like Teddy did. What is for certain is that the current candidates running for the Presidency just want to be President. They'll roll over for elites to get there. That is why America could turn to you despite the differences of opinions in how they view you. It is my belief Americans who have been left behind are *Seeing 2020* already and believe you may be their best shot for change. Benjamin Franklin believed in the gut instinct of the American people. I do as well. I believe they will make the right call concerning *The Big Picture* come election day.

Sincerely,

Don Beaudoin Jr. (P/N)

References (Bibliography)

AEI. (2018). Dynamic chart: World's ten largest economies, 1961 to 2017
http://www.aei.org/publication/dynamic-graph-of-the-day-top-ten-countries-by-
gdp-1961-to-2017/

Berkowitz, B., Alcantara, C. and Lu, D. The terrible numbers that grow with each
mass shooting. Retrieved from
https://www.washingtonpost.com/graphics/2018/national/mass-shootings-in-
america/?noredirect=on

Budget of the United States Government. Retrieved from
https://www.govinfo.gov/app/collection/budget/

Bowman, J. (Revised Edition 2002). The History of the American Presidency.
Revised Edition. World Publications Group, Inc.

Calamur, K. The Atlantic. (2018). Oil Was Supposed to Rebuild Iraq. Conflict and
politics got in the way. Retrieved from
https://www.theatlantic.com/international/archive/2018/03/iraq-oil/555827/

Centers for Disease Control and Prevention. (2019). Tobacco Use. Retrieved from
https://www.cdc.gov/chronicdisease/resources/publications/factsheets/tobacco.ht
m

CPI Inflation Calculator. (2019). Retrieved from https://data.bls.gov/cgi-
bin/cpicalc.pl?cost1=5100&year1=201801&year2=201201

Congressional Research Service. (2018). Infrastructure Investment and the Federal
Government. Retrieved from https://fas.org/sgp/crs/misc/IF10592.pdf

Congressional Research Service. (2019). Mexico: Organized Crime and Drug Trafficking Organizations. Retrieved from https://fas.org/sgp/crs/row/R41576.pdf

Cox, J. (2015). Number of Deaths Caused by Marijuana Much More than Zero. Retrieved from https://familycouncil.org/?p=11795

Derysh, I. (2019). Joe Biden to rich donors: "Nothing would fundamentally change" if he's elected. Retrieved from https://www.salon.com/2019/06/19/joe-biden-to-rich-donors-nothing-would-fundamentally-change-if-hes-elected/

Dobbs, L. & Wright, M. FOX News Network Video. (2017, September 18). DOJ Investigating possible insider trading by Equifax executives. Retrieved from https://www.msn.com/en-us/money/news/doj-investigating-possible-insider-trading-by-equifax-executives/vi-AAsbglu

EPA.gov. (2017). EPA's Administrator Scott Pruitt. Retrieved from https://www.epa.gov/aboutepa/epas-administrator

Federal Poverty Guidelines. Retrieved from https://familiesusa.org/product/federal-poverty-guidelines

Federal Poverty Level. Retrieved from https://www.healthcare.gov/glossary/federal-poverty-level-fpl/

Finnegan, W. (2014). Demonizing the Minimum Wage. Retrieved from https://www.newyorker.com/news/daily-comment/demonizing-minimum-wage

Fitzgerald, M. CNBC.com. The CEOs of nearly 200 companies just said shareholder value is no longer their main objective. Retrieved from https://www.cnbc.com/2019/08/19/the-ceos-of-nearly-two-hundred-companies-say-shareholder-value-is-no-longer-their-main-objective.html

Geere, D. (2011). How the first cable was laid across the Atlantic. Retrieved from http://www.wired.co.uk/article/transatlantic-cables

George, Patrick. (2013). Women Get $4.2 Million After Truck Shot By LAPD During Manhunt. Retrieved from https://jalopnik.com/women-whose-truck-was-shot-by-lapd-awarded-4-2-million-479483148

Golden mean (philosophy). (2017). New World Encyclopedia. Retrieved from http://www.newworldencyclopedia.org/p/index.php?title=Golden_mean_(philosophy)&oldid=1005352

History.com (2018). Oil Industry. Retrieved from https://www.history.com/topics/industrial-revolution/oil-industry

Hodgekiss, A. & Spencer, B. DailyMail.com. (2016, February 23). EXCLUSIVE: How Big Pharma greed is killing tens of thousands around the world: Patients are over-medicated and often given profitable drugs with 'little proven benefits,' leading doctors warn. Retrieved from http://www.dailymail.co.uk/health/article-3460321/How-Big-Pharma-greed-killing-tens-thousands-world-Patients-medicated-given-profitable-drugs-little-proven-benefits-leading-doctors-warn.html

HRC CaDS Section 19932. (2015). Dan Brown's inferno and population growth. Retrieved from http://www.britishempire.co.uk/science/communications/telegraph.htm

Hughes, Matthew. 'Collateral Damage' and the Battle for Saipan, 1944 https://tandfonline.com/doi/abs/10.1080/03071840802670148?src=recsys&journalCode=rusi20

IET (The Institution of Engineering and Technology). (2017). The first transatlantic telegraph cable 1858. Retrieved from http://www.theiet.org/resources/library/archives/featured/trans-cable1858.cfm

International Monetary Fund. IMF DataMapper. (2019). Retrieved from https://www.imf.org/external/datamapper/NGDPD@WEO/OEMDC/ADVEC/WEO/JPN/FRA

"It ain't over 'til it's over" ("It's not over until it's over"). Retrieved from https://www.barrypopik.com/index.php/new_york_city/entry/it_aint_over_til_its_over

Kopf, D. (2019). THE SPOILS OF TRADE WAR: Mexico is finally the US's number-one trading partner. Retrieved from https://qz.com/1682861/mexico-is-now-americas-number-one-trading-partner/

Lascomba, S. Britishempire.co.uk. Spanning the continents telegraphy. Retrieved from http://www.britishempire.co.uk/science/communications/telegraph.htm

Macfarlane, A. (2017, May 19). China makes 'flammable ice' breakthrough in South China Sea. Retrieved from http://money.cnn.com/2017/05/19/news/china-flammable-ice-sea/index.html

Mayne, Melanie. (2013, March 29). The origin of the American Democratic Party. Retrieved from http://www.todayifoundout.com/index.php/2013/03/the-origin-of-the-american-democratic-party/

Mitchell, Margaret. (1936). Macmillan Publishing Company. GONE WITH THE WIND.

Morrison, Sara. (2014). Police Officers Who Shot at Two Innocent Women 103 Times Won't Be Fired. Retrieved from https://www.theatlantic.com/national/archive/2014/02/police-officers-who-shot-two-innocent-women-103-times-wont-be-fired/357771/

Mass Shootings. Retrieved from https://www.washingtonpost.com/graphics/2018/national/mass-shootings-in-america/?noredirect=on

Mazzetti, M., Goldman, A., Schmidt, M. & Apuzzo, M. (2017, May 20). NYtimes.com. Killing C.I.A. informants, China crippled U.S. spying operations. Retrieved from https://www.nytimes.com/2017/05/20/world/asia/china-cia-spies-espionage.html

McCarthy, N. (2019). The Number Of U.S. Police Officers Killed In The Line Of Duty Increased Last Year. Retrieved from https://www.forbes.com/sites/niallmccarthy/2019/05/08/the-number-of-u-s-police-officers-killed-in-the-line-of-duty-increased-last-year-infographic/#6e28b82c1189

Morner, N. (2015, November 19). The approaching new grand solar minimum and little ice age climate conditions. Retrieved from http://file.scirp.org/pdf/NS_2015111916552083.pdf

National Institute of Alcohol Related Deaths and Alcoholism. (2019). Retrieved from https://www.niaaa.nih.gov/alcohol-facts-and-statistics

Needleman, H. (1999, June 28). The removal of lead from gasoline: Historical and personal reflection. Retrieved from https://www.unc.edu/courses/2007fall/envr/230/001/Needleman_2000.pdf

Noack, R. (2015, September 24). The future of language. Retrieved from https://www.washingtonpost.com/news/worldviews/wp/2015/09/24/the-future-of-language/?utm_term=.e7b149ea0439

Oyez.org. Citizens United v. Federal Election Commission. Retrieved from https://www.oyez.org/cases/2008/08-205

Oyez.org. Planned Parenthood of Southeastern Pennsylvania v. Casey. Retrieved from Oyez.org/cases/1991/91-744

Perlez, J. & Huang, Y. (2017, May 13). Behind China's $1trillion plan to shake up the economic order. Retrieved from https://www.nytimes.com/2017/05/13/business/china-railway-one-belt-one-road-1-trillion-plan.html

Pach Jr., C. Dwight D. Eisenhower: Life in Brief. Retrieved from https://millercenter.org/president/eisenhower/life-in-brief

Pinker, S. & Mack, A. Slate.com. (2014, December 22). The world is not falling apart. Retrieved from http://www.slate.com/articles/news_and_politics/foreigners/2014/12/the_world_is_not_falling_apart_the_trend_lines_reveal_an_increasingly_peaceful.html

QuoteInvestigation.com. Your liberty to swing your fist ends just where my nose begins. Retrieved from https://quoteinvestigator.com/2011/10/15/liberty-fist-nose/

Radford, B. (2019). Who Are Mass Shooters? Mass Shooter Demographics. Retrieved from https://centerforinquiry.org/blog/who-are-mass-shooters-mass-shooter-demographics-part-2/

Sampat, P. (2001). Last Words. Excerpted from May/June 2001 WORLD WATCH. Retrieved from http://www.worldwatch.org/system/files/EP143A.pdf

Schulze, E. (2018). 3 charts that show why the US should stop ignoring its debt problem. Retrieved from
https://www.cnbc.com/2018/07/26/3-charts-that-show-why-the-us-should-stop-ignoring-its-debt-problem.html

Shutterstock.com. (2019). By cherezoff. Royalty-free stock illustration ID: 793033303. Planet Earth with a spectacular sunset - North America. Elements of this image furnished by NASA. 3d illustration – Illustration. Retrieved from https://www.shutterstock.com/image-illustration/planet-earth-spectacular-sunset-north-america-793033303

Statista Research Department. Percentage of households in the United States owning one or more firearms from 1972 to 2018.
Retrieved from
https://www.statista.com/statistics/249740/percentage-of-households-in-the-united-states-owning-a-firearm/

The Planetary Society. (2019). Light Sail: Flight by light for cubesats. Retrieved from http://www.planetary.org/explore/projects/lightsail-solar-sailing/

The telegraphic messages of Queen Victoria and President Buchanan.
Retrieved from http://atlantic-cable.com/Article/1858Leslies/0828a.jpg

The Top One Percent. Retrieved from
https://dqydj.com/top-one-percent-united-states/

TIME Magazine, Reissue of TIME'S Special Edition. Founding Fathers. The American Visionaries Who Created a Nation. (2019).

Tseng, Nin-Hai. Fortune.com. (2013, September 11). Retrieved from http://fortune.com/2013/09/11/the-rich-got-a-lot-richer-since-the-financial-crisis/

United Nations Department of Economic and Social Affairs. (2017). World
population projected to reach 9.8 billion in 2050, and 11.2 billion in 2100.
Retrieved from
https://www.un.org/development/desa/en/news/population/world-population-
prospects-2017.html

United Nations. DESA / Population Division: World Population Prospects 2019.
(2019). Retrieved from
https://population.un.org/wpp/Download/Standard/Population/

U.S. Population Growth Rate By Year. Retrieved from
https://www.multpl.com/us-population-growth-rate/table/by-year

US population growth hits 80-year low, capping off a year of demographic
stagnation. Retrieved from
https://www.brookings.edu/blog/the-avenue/2018/12/21/us-population-growth-
hits-80-year-low-capping-off-a-year-of-demographic-stagnation/

U.S. Department of Labor (2019). History of Federal Minimum Wage Rates
Under the Fair Labor Standards Act, 1938 – 2009. Retrieved from
https://www.dol.gov/whd/minwage/chart.htm

Webb, W. (2019). Israel's Secretive Nuclear Facility Leaking as Watchdog Finds
Israel Has Nearly 100 Nukes. Retrieved from
https://www.mintpressnews.com/international-watchdog-finds-israel-has-nearly-
100-nuclear-weapons/259274/

WhiteHouse.gov. (2018). FACT SHEET 2018 BUDGET: INFRASTRUCTURE
INITIATIVE. Retrieved from
https://www.whitehouse.gov/sites/whitehouse.gov/files/omb/budget/fy2018/fact_s
heets/2018%20Budget%20Fact%20Sheet_Infrastructure%20Initiative1.pdf

Wikipedia. Haditha Massacre. Retrieved from
https://en.wikipedia.org/wiki/Haditha_massacre

Wikipedia. Joint Strike Fighter Program. Retrieved from
https://en.wikipedia.org/wiki/Lockheed_Martin_F-35_Lightning_II

Wikipedia. NASA spinoff technologies. Retrieved from
https://en.wikipedia.org/wiki/NASA_spinoff_technologies

Wolchover, N. (2012, September 24). Why did the Democratic and Republican
Parties Switch Platforms? Retrieved from
https://www.livescience.com/34241-democratic-republican-parties-switch-
platforms.html

World Inequality Report, Executive Summary. (2018). Top One Percent versus
bottom 50%. Retrieved from
https://wir2018.wid.world/files/download/wir2018-summary-english.pdf